Praise for
The Power of Collective Wisdom

Leadership and Organizational Development

"An extraordinary book filled with powerful insights, evocative stories, and yes, collective wisdom! Beyond the Knowledge Revolution lies the Wisdom Revolution—and this book points the way."
—William Ury, coauthor of *Getting to Yes*; author of *The Third Side: Why We Fight and How We Can Stop*; and cofounder, Harvard Law School's Program on Negotiation

"This is an exceptional work challenging leaders to question their assumptions about how to achieve organizational excellence and providing a new narrative for leading with an eye toward collective wisdom. I love this book's message that we are all needed and that each of us has a reason to invest in one another."
—Carol Pearson, PhD, Executive Vice President and Provost, Pacifica Graduate Institute, and author of *The Hero Within*

"What I find especially useful about this book is that along with its creativity in search of wisdom is its inclusion of humanities' destructive inclinations, what the authors call *collective folly*. Decision makers and leaders will find this book a necessary stop in any search for wisdom."
—Arthur D. Colman, MD, author of *Up from Scapegoating*; Senior Fellow, James MacGregor Burns Academy of Leadership; and Clinical Professor, UC San Francisco Medical Center, San Francisco

"*The Power of Collective Wisdom* is down to earth, extremely practical, and rich with wisdom—a rare combination. It shows how collaboration is possible and necessary for those who care deeply about the outcome of their collective efforts. The book is remarkably easy to read but also reaches a depth of thought that is engaging and profound."
—Jan Boller, PhD, RN, Associate Professor and Director of Nursing Leadership Programs, College of Graduate Nursing, Western University of Health Sciences, and coauthor of *Daily Miracles*

"The most significant challenges of our time—social, economic, and environmental—are calling for leaders to understand, trust, and draw upon relational and cocreative capacities. This inspiring and practical book points the way. Not only have authors Briskin, Erikson, Ott, and Callanan written about collective wisdom, they have created it."

—Diana Whitney, PhD, author of *The Power of Appreciative Inquiry*

"In a time when expressions like 'wisdom of the crowd' can be shorthand for quick, uninformed group decision making, *The Power of Collective Wisdom* gives the world a new vocabulary to distinguish the various states and stages of wisdom. Finally, a book that explains what collective wisdom is and how to harness this wisdom if we hope to survive as a species!"

—Peter Coughlan, Partner and Coleader of
Transformation Practice, IDEO

Community and Institutional Renewal

"This book takes knowledge about groups and elevates it to a field and a movement. The authors are original thinkers and good writers and have the ability to integrate a breadth of thinking into a new whole."

—Peter Block, author of *Community* and *Stewardship*

"In this time of challenge and change, we need to have hope. People everywhere, from the lowest caste in India to the highest penthouse in New York's Upper East Side, are seeking wisdom. This book maps the territory and points toward a new field of knowing, where together we can effectively explore possible solutions. Indeed, *The Power of Collective Wisdom* may be the most important book of our times."

—Michael Toms, CEO, New Dimensions Media, and author of
A Time for Choices: Deep Dialogues for Deep Democracy and
An Open Life: Joseph Campbell in Conversation with Michael Toms

"I think we are all seeing the growing need and yearning for approaches that enable people to think wisely together about critical issues and concerns. This pioneering book helps illuminate the lived experience of collective wisdom and invites us to create the conditions that make its appearance more likely. It is a great contribution to both theory and practice in this rapidly growing field."

—Juanita Brown and David Isaacs, cofounders,
The World Café, and coauthors of *The World Café*

"This book is a timely reminder that whenever two or more are gathered, there is *always* the potential for wisdom as well as folly. We owe the authors a debt of gratitude for providing signposts to recognize when we are slipping into folly and practices to help us create conditions that support collective creativity, inspiration, and wise choices."

—Glenna Gerard, coauthor of *Dialogue: Rediscover the Transforming
Power of Conversation,* and creator of The Presence Walkabout

"These days more and more of us need to act together decisively and still avoid folly. *The Power of Collective Wisdom* provides anyone who is part of a group confronting a crisis with practical approaches for finding the 'sweet spot' where the group's best potential can be realized."

—Marvin Southard, DSW, Director, Los Angeles County
Department of Mental Health

Social Justice and Environmental Activism

"This book confirmed what I have learned from my peace-building work in Kenya. The conceptual framework provided helps to free us from thinking that narrows our scope to one that broadens our understanding. It asks us to seek individual and collective empowerment of people and institutions—recognizing that the answer does not lie within an individual or an organization but through linking periphery and center, top to bottom, and sectors of society together."

—Dekha Ibrahim Abdi, peace activist and recipient
of the 2007 Right Livelihood Award

"We at PeaceJam have been bringing Nobel Peace Laureates together for a series of dialogues. The collective moral and spiritual voice that has emerged from our dialogues was made possible by the base of knowledge provided by the Collective Wisdom Initiative and now this book. *The Power of Collective Wisdom* is valuable for anyone working to find common ground in groups, whether that be at the highest levels of peace negotiations or at the grassroots level of community organizing and youth education."

—Dawn Engle, cofounder and Director, PeaceJam

"In an era that desperately needs more comprehensive solutions, this book challenges traditional views of where wisdom resides, shifting us from the individual to the whole. This transformative process both embraces many voices and embodies deep insight for outcomes that are more connective, more intelligent, and more complete."

—Rev. angel Kyodo williams, author of *Being Black: Zen and the Art of Living with Fearlessness and Grace*, and founder, Center for Transformative Change

"The complexity and urgency of today's environmental challenges will not be solved by experts, politicians, activists, and others working in isolation. Real breakthroughs arise only when stakeholders agree to have conversations about controversial issues with new, open attitudes. This book is a must-read for anyone looking to get beyond the either/or mind-set and help divergent groups of people to collaborate and innovate together."

—Diane Demee-Benoit, Director of Programs, Institute at the Golden Gate

"I wish I had this book five or ten years ago; I'm thrilled to have it now. Many of us in social justice work wonder why we can't always maximize our common strength, passion, and potential. *The Power of Collective Wisdom* powerfully and carefully explores what we need to crack the code. It paints a compelling picture—compassionately but without sentimentality—of the traps we fall into and the alternative possibilities that are within our grasp. If we can absorb the lessons of this timely resource and begin to integrate them with more courage, wondrous things will likely be the result."

—Claudia Horwitz, Executive Director, stone circles and
The Stone House, and author of *The Spiritual Activist*

Spiritual and Religious Traditions

"A fascinating account of a meeting between ancient wisdom traditions and contemporary challenges. It shows how dialogue, reflection, and higher purpose can help us reimagine groups and larger collectives so that they can be a force for healing and repair—*together we can get it together.* The book is a call for all who wish to contribute to the health of their communities, organizations, and planet through a deeper connection to their own talents, vision, and spirit."

—Reb Zalman Schachter-Shalomi, Professor Emeritus, Temple
University; World Wisdom Chair, Naropa University; founder,
Alliance for Jewish Renewal; and author of *From Age-ing to Sage-ing*

"*The Power of Collective Wisdom* accelerates a movement that is quietly on the rise during this time of vast cultural change. This book names it, outlines the thinkers and leaders, and distinguishes—through real-life stories and fables—collective wisdom from groupthink gone awry. It will expand your grasp of the role of groups to re-envision the inclusive, peaceful, creative world we all long for."

—Lauren Artress, Episcopal priest; author of *Walking a Sacred Path:
Rediscovering the Labyrinth as a Spiritual Tool*; and founder
and Creative Director, Veriditas

"While many romanticize either the lone individual or the community, *The Power of Collective Wisdom* understands the essential complexity of a freely formed association of individuals who listen deeply, speak truly, and act ethically. If we are to attain the essential insights required for our future, we will need each other. Where old forms of community fail us, we need new spiritually sound forms suited to our collective future."

—Arthur Zajonc, Professor of Physics, Amherst College,
and Scientific Coordinator, Mind and Life Dialogues
with His Holiness the Dalai Lama

"This sourcebook teaches us to recognize the ingredients and skills that can bring collective wisdom to the forefront of human endeavor. The authors reveal that just as intentional and disciplined use of these ingredients and skills gives rise to creative actions, ignoring them reinforces the folly of separation and sectarianism. This unique work shows that we ourselves are responsible for committing to collective wisdom and caring in order to harness our human potential to heal the earth and benefit all of humanity."
—Roshi Wendy Egyoku Nakao, Zen Center of Los Angeles

"*The Power of Collective Wisdom* is a meditation, a journey, and a pragmatic investigation of a worldview that challenges all individuals and organizations to open to their potential for collective wisdom. The authors reveal the power of the emergence of group wisdom through a variety of stories and illustrations, offering a workable solution to many of today's conflicts. It is an ideal read for managers, politicians, health and human service workers, teachers, coaches, parents, and those who wish to remember how good it is to be a human being, connected to other human beings, the Creator, and the earth."
—Francesca Mason Boring, Shoshone, author of *Feather Medicine: Walking in Shoshone Dreamtime*, and facilitator/teacher of Family, Human, and Natural Systems Constellation

the power of
COLLECTIVE
WISDOM

And the Trap of
Collective Folly

Alan Briskin	Sheryl Erickson	John Ott	Tom Callanan

BK

Berrett–Koehler Publishers, Inc.
San Francisco

Berrett-Koehler Publishers, Inc.
235 Montgomery Street, Suite 650
San Francisco, CA 94104-2916
Tel: (415) 288-0260   Fax: (415) 362-2512   www.bkconnection.com

Ordering Information
Quantity sales. Special discounts are available on quantity purchases by corporations, associations, and others. For details, contact the "Special Sales Department" at the Berrett-Koehler address above.
Individual sales. Berrett-Koehler publications are available through most bookstores. They can also be ordered directly from Berrett-Koehler: Tel: (800) 929-2929; Fax: (802) 864-7626; www.bkconnection.com
Orders for college textbook/course adoption use. Please contact Berrett-Koehler: Tel: (800) 929-2929; Fax: (802) 864-7626.
Orders by U.S. trade bookstores and wholesalers. Please contact Ingram Publisher Services, Tel: (800) 509-4887; Fax: (800) 838-1149; E-mail: customer.service@ingrampublisherservices.com; or visit www.ingrampublisherservices.com/Ordering for details about electronic ordering.

Berrett-Koehler and the BK logo are registered trademarks of Berrett-Koehler Publishers, Inc.

Printed in the United States of America
Berrett-Koehler books are printed on long-lasting acid-free paper. When it is available, we choose paper that has been manufactured by environmentally responsible processes. These may include using trees grown in sustainable forests, incorporating recycled paper, minimizing chlorine in bleaching, or recycling the energy produced at the paper mill.

Library of Congress Cataloging-in-Publication Data
The power of collective wisdom and the trap of collective folly / Alan Briskin ...
[et al.]. — 1st ed.
   p. cm.
Includes bibliographical references and index.
ISBN 978-1-57675-445-0 (pbk.)
1. Group decision making. 2. Consensus (Social sciences) 3. Leadership. I. Briskin, Alan, 1954–
HM746.P68 2009
302.3'5—dc22   2009012642

First Edition
15 14 13 12 11 10 09   10 9 8 7 6 5 4 3 2 1

INTERIOR DESIGN: Laura Lind Design   COVER DESIGN: Silverleaf Design
COPY EDITOR: Elissa Rabellino   PROOFREADER: Henrietta Bensussen
PRODUCTION: Linda Jupiter Productions   INDEXER: Carol Frenier

Contents

Foreword
by Peter Senge

Few words have a longer historical association with leadership than wisdom, and few have less credibility in that association today.

What has happened?

First, it seems that we have lost our consensual definition of what wisdom actually is. In earlier eras, when elders had revered places in community, we had a way of understanding wisdom through example. The elders grounded us in appreciating the importance of perspective, in seeing things from multiple points of view, in considering what the past could teach us about the future, and in reminding us that many things we might think were our own unique problems had in fact been faced by others before and we should meditate on what we could learn from that.

Second, in an era that has little deep concern about the future, wisdom has little functional value. For wisdom has always been concerned with balancing the short term and the long term—of seeing possible longer-term consequences of our actions in and for the future.

But for most of us most of the time, the future does not really exist. Indeed, an important feature of the modern era has been the marginalization of the future. The future has become an abstraction rather than a reality with which we are emotionally connected. An economist's prediction. A futurist's fantasy images. A few more technological gadgets.

Something that will come someday but is of little importance in shaping the decisions we make today. Spend now, pay later. Get the stock price as high as possible so that your public stock offering brings in as much money as possible. Live for the moment. The future will take care of itself. The end of history (and, by implication, the end of the future).

All of this seemed to work so long as people could basically assume that the future was more or less an extrapolation of the past, just with another 3 percent of GDP growth and more technology.

But then that complacency started to wear thin. Gradually, a deep and pervasive anxiety about the future began to set in. Climate change. Food safety. Pollution. Toxicity in everyday products (and more and more people getting cancers at younger and younger ages). The gap between rich and poor. Social and political instability. Terrorism.

Today, according to a Gallup Poll, two-thirds of sixteen- to twenty-four-year-olds in America believe the world was a better place when their parents were their age—and over half are convinced it will be worse for their own children. With this pessimism has come historically low confidence ratings for virtually all the primary institutions that shape modern society: business, investors, public education, health care, Congress.

So now, wisdom may be making a comeback—if it weren't for the fact that most people seem to regard it as a thing of bygone eras, a sort of historical footnote, or maybe myth, that is so antithetical to how we think and act today that the phrase *wise leadership* seems almost an oxymoron.

That is why this book is so important.

First, it corrects a basic misconception, that wisdom is not developable. Coming from diverse contemplative traditions, the authors bridge modern challenges with ancient understandings of how wisdom can be cultivated: through continual reflection, through silence, and through connecting with the highest in yourself and others.

Second is that wisdom is not about just a few wise people but about the capacity of human communities to make wise choices and to orient themselves around a living sense of the future that truly matters to them. Wisdom is about connection, connection to one another and to a larger whole. It is an inherently relational concept and founders when we overidentify it with particular people.

While the world's cultures offer a rich storehouse of stories of extraordinary individuals who exercised wisdom, upon closer inspection what makes the stories compelling is what emerged collectively. Gandhi and Martin Luther King Jr. were not wise leaders just because of what they said but also because of the coordinated and consequential actions they helped inspire among millions. But even these examples are misleading, insofar as they start with the central leadership figure. For it is the everyday emergence of collective intelligence in teams, communities, and networks that is most relevant for today.

Marianne Knuth, cofounder of Kufunda Village, a network of sustainable agriculture villages in Zimbabwe, and of Pioneers of Change, one of many extraordinary global youth leadership networks tackling the most pressing issues of our time, expresses this sensibility of action for the whole in criticizing why most direct aid efforts to address poverty fail:

The development sector is still engaged in a large-scale mechanistic and hierarchical approach to addressing the challenges of poverty and so-called under-development. In the name of material development, villages and communities have to adopt less communal ways of relating to each other. In the name of development, problems are fixed for a community without recognizing the need for ownership in the development initiative by the community itself.

The consequence is that "larger scale development initiatives fix a problem for a short term, only to have the problem return years later (abandoned boreholes, broken down toilets, or community pumps for which no one has taken ownership after the intervener has left)."[1]

Third, the authors show that rather than being a "feel good" concept with little tangible impact, wisdom is all about results, and especially what is achieved over the longer term. Groups dedicated to developing collective wisdom can have dramatically greater effectiveness in what they achieve. Throughout this book are examples of how collective wisdom arises and is shaped precisely through people's engagement with real problems, and through learning how to achieve lasting outcomes that matter.

In this process of engaging real problems, a subtlety also emerges that distinguishes collective wisdom from other, more common forms of intelligence. The world is full of smart people. Every failed third world developmental program, every failed corporate strategy, every disastrous national policy was designed by smart people. The real distinction between wisdom and the types of intelligence that abound in modern society comes from not knowing the answers. Wisdom manifests in humility rather than arrogance. It is known by its quiet presence rather than by noisy advocacy for one way. In this sense, collective wisdom is much more about the capacity for learning than about a single brilliant decision.

All learning arises through doing, but the most frequent problem is the "learning," not the "doing." Our organizations and societies are full of doing but deficient in learning. I believe there is no more telling indicator of the absence of collective wisdom than the inability to learn as we go. It is characterized by rigidness and dogma. It is characterized by low trust and the inability to talk about difficult subjects where people must recognize their shortfalls. It is characterized by maintaining a façade of confidence and competence that masks insecurity and fear of failure. Conversely, collective wisdom is most evident in quiet confidence that our "not knowing" is our strength, that the ability to ask deep questions is more important than offering superficial answers— and that imagination, commitment, patience and openness, and trust in one another will consistently trump IQ over the long haul.

Why does all this matter, especially today? Because the problems we face today do not have "right answers." Our most pressing problems are characterized by unprecedented levels of complexity and interdependence, and the consequent breakdown of the conventional problem-solving paradigm. The well-known conflict resolution facilitator Mark Gerzon says in this book, "Humanity is hungering for wisdom. That is the word I hear most: not *compassion*; not *love*; not *peace*; not *kindness*—but *wisdom*." This is precisely be-cause we sense that the major challenges we face will not be solved by a few more smart people or technological magic bullets.

Lastly, because of this urgency, what matters most today is not only to clarify what wisdom is and why it matters, but to understand how to go about developing collective wis-dom. That is why the most important contribution of this book is not just pointing out that wisdom is developable, but offering stories and practices that can help each of us in our own wisdom journey.

In our work, we have come to see this journey revolv-ing around three intertwined openings, what Otto Scharmer terms opening the mind, opening the heart, and opening the will.[2] These three openings are each evident in the stories and practices presented in the pages that follow: learning how to listen more deeply and suspend our taken-for-granted mental models, how to connect with one another in that listening, and, perhaps quietly and barely noticed, how to pay atten-tion to why we are here.

Reflecting on her journey, Knuth says simply, "In the be-ginning was the meeting. . . . How we meet people deter-mines all else. Do we meet people assuming the best we can about them? Do we meet each person curious about the mir-acle of a human being that we are about to connect with? Or do we meet a *poor* person that we are about to help?"

She tells a story of Anna, a widow of forty-six who lives on a $2 per month pension from her late husband but must pay $20 every three months in children's school fees. Despite these hardships, Anna set up a women's crochet cooperative, started teaching knitting to women in her area, built her own compost toilet and taught others how to do the same, and now runs an AIDS dialogue group and provides home care for AIDS patients. Asked how all this was possible, Anna says, "I have learnt that I have been an example in my community for being a widowed woman who overcame severe hardship. I have learnt that I am a strong woman. I have learnt that I can find peace of mind within myself. I have learnt that I am a good listener, and I am trustworthy." Knuth adds, "I do not understand how all of these things are happening. But I do know that we met Anna *in her wisdom*. Not in her poverty."[3]

For me, the promise of this work is that we all learn more and more how to meet one another in our wisdom. Then our challenges will appear not as threats to our way of life but as opportunities to grow into life itself.

—Peter M. Senge

Founding chair, Society for Organizational Learning

Senior Lecturer, MIT Sloan School of Management

Author of *The Fifth Discipline* and coauthor of *Presence*

and *The Necessary Revolution*.

Welcome

This book is intended for people who seek more effective and satisfying ways of working with others. It is for people who are working to make their communities, neighborhoods, and organizations more inclusive, effective, and wise. Everyone who participates in groups has something important to contribute and something further to learn. As authors, we bring to bear our learning from decades of convening groups and participating in large-scale change efforts in business, health care, education, mental health, criminal justice, conflict resolution, and global initiatives. Ten years ago, we founded and have since shepherded the Collective Wisdom Initiative, an informal network of practitioners and scholars from around the world who are bringing together a body of research, theory, and practice into a field of study that we have come to call *collective wisdom*.

Collective wisdom refers to knowledge and insight gained through group and community interaction. At a deeper level, however, it is about our living connection to each other and the interdependence we share in our neighborhoods, organizations, and world community. Supported by the Fetzer Institute, a private operating foundation in Kalamazoo, Michigan, the Collective Wisdom Initiative shares with Fetzer a common conviction: that efforts to address the world's critical issues must go beyond political, social, and economic strategies to their psychological, spiritual, and cultural roots. Behind our shared conviction lies a belief that human survival depends upon our recognizing that we have a stake in each other's well-being, and that groups have potential for being sources of extraordinary creative power, incubators of innovative ideas, and vehicles for social healing.

The Power of Collective Wisdom is the result of a collaboration involving dozens of contributors and hundreds of people from our network and beyond. Stories fill the book, telling of collective wisdom's emergence in diverse settings, across different cultures, and in earlier times. Our book outlines the commitments and convictions that aid collective wisdom's emergence in groups. It also sketches a larger worldview, one encompassing the reverence for life associated with wisdom and the importance of a collective perspective. Throughout these pages, readers will be guided toward a deeper understanding of the conditions that make wisdom possible in groups and the characteristics that underlie many successful group methodologies.

We also offer a caution. We need to be alert to wisdom's opposing potential. One of the main messages of the book is just how easy it is to fall into the trap of *collective folly* instead of collective wisdom. This happens when groups, organizations, or communities become so polarized that they can't see the consequences of their collective actions. Similarly, false or forced agreement in groups can lead to tragic consequences. The power of collective wisdom is furthered when we learn how to navigate skillfully between the shores of polarization and false agreement.

We see our efforts as part of a larger social movement. Everywhere we look, we see groups, networks, and communities rising up to address common challenges. What all of us share is a collective outlook and a desire for wise action. We seek what human beings have always sought: to find what is best in ourselves and what is best in and for the group. Our intent in the following pages is to articulate some of the key ideas of this search and to provide a foundation for the field of collective wisdom's further development.

Use of Terms

COLLECTIVE — A number of persons or things considered as one group or whole; marked by connection among or with the members of a group.

FOLLY — Lacking good sense or normal prudence and foresight, a continuum of behaviors ranging from personally foolish behavior to criminality, evil, and depravity.

POWER — The ability, strength, and capacity to do something, including the capacity to bring about change.

TRAP — Something by which one is caught or stopped unawares; a position or situation from which it is difficult or impossible to escape.

WISDOM — Exercising sound judgment; reflects great understanding of people and of situations. Considerate of multiple perspectives and forms of intelligence. Wisdom in groups is demonstrated by insight, good sense, clarity, objectivity, and discernment rooted in deep caring and compassion.

Collective and Wisdom Makes the Difference

It started with a bolt of lightning in an area of wilderness known as Mann Gulch in Montana. In a telling case study of collective failure, twelve young smokejumpers and a forest ranger lost their lives battling the flames that erupted. Everything that could have gone wrong that tragic day seemed to, including the final moments when an action was taken that might have saved them. Wagner Dodge, who headed the crew, came up with a brilliant tactic. As the flames from the fire whipped their way toward the men, he bent down and lit a fire to the grass in front of him. As the fire spread, it burned in a widening circle. Standing in front of this wall of flame, he stepped through onto a small charred patch of ground that allowed him to "hide" within the larger body of the blaze. This was not a *backfire*, in which an area of ground is burned in front of an oncoming blaze to create a firebreak. There was no time. This was simply a case of an in-the-moment reaction.

From within the burned-out patch of ground, Dodge beckoned the two men closest to him to follow him in. They could not hear him amid the sounds of exploding trees and screaming winds, but they could see him frantically waving, motioning them to follow him inside the circle. Instead, they glanced his way and kept going. And then the rest of the men passed by, not one of them following their crew chief into the safety of the circle. With the exception of Dodge and two men who miraculously stumbled into an area barren of vegetation, everyone perished. It was the worst disaster in Forest Service history.

There were certainly lessons here about leadership, especially in this particular circumstance, which later documented failed relationships among the crew and a command-and-control style of leadership. There were also lessons about the need for cooperation, trust, teamwork, and coordination, lessons the Forest Service took seriously and which transformed their ways of preparing teams rather than just individuals.[1] Yet, at a deeper level, there is a more fundamental question. What allows us, in groups and larger collectives, to find solutions amid complexity and daunting circumstances, to make wise choices and work together, as opposed to splintering apart and failing to see what opportunities arise? How can we *together* find solutions to pressing and bewildering problems that face us every day? How can we know when and how to join with others, stepping through fire if necessary?

The failure at Mann Gulch was not due to any one element alone; the science of firefighting was at an early stage, wind direction is always unpredictable, and bad luck played its part. We all understand how external conditions can dictate the outcome of a situation. What stood out, however, from the studies that followed was something internal to the group. There had been an assumption, which proved tragic, that men individually trained, put on a plane without even knowing each other, and given orders to obey their crew chief without question would know what to do when their circumstances changed dramatically. There had been precious little understanding about how to prepare groups to improvise when necessary and trust in each other.

The lessons learned from Mann Gulch were not a call for just any change, but for a change in thinking about how to save lives. The tragedy moved the Forest Service in the direction of thinking collectively: how to train men together and create greater collaboration among the various disciplines involved with fire safety. They dedicated themselves to the question of how best to make sound judgments as teams and to cultivate the intelligence that existed from the bottom up, from the smokejumpers and firefighters who fought the fires. It is a lesson we must now learn on a much larger scale.

The Power of Collective Wisdom is a call for people to come together to think collectively about the circumstances they face. It is a guide to reclaiming our participation in groups as positive, necessary, and hopeful without sugarcoating the external challenges we face or the internal obstacles that prevent us from seeing new possibilities. Wisdom reflects a capacity for sound judgment, discernment, and the objectivity to see what is needed in the moment. Collective wisdom reflects a similar capacity to learn together and evolve toward something greater and wiser than what we can do as individuals alone. This book emerges from a deep conviction that we have a stake in each other and that what binds us together is greater than what drives us apart.

THE NEED FOR THIS BOOK

We must find insight and ways to cooperate with each other at a depth and scale that is unprecedented. We see this need appearing everywhere—on the front pages of our newspapers, in our organizations, and even within our network of family and friends. If we cannot find legitimate ways to join together, to cooperate and to understand each other, we will not find solutions to the dysfunctionality and messes that seem to be growing all around us, let alone to the largest problems that beset us as nations and as a world community, such as global warming, poverty, and war.

We cannot any longer

- kill our way out of it,
- deny that it is happening, or
- rationalize that this is just the way it is.

If we do not turn the temperature down, literally and figuratively, on the global challenges we face and the polarization and fragmentation we live with on a daily basis, we will be staring down a path of untenable choices. Are we willing to gamble our future and our children's future on more of the same?

Change happens on a macro systems level but also on a micro level—one conversation at a time, one group at a time, one new idea spawned among a group of committed people, setting off a chain reaction of new possibilities. We believe this kind of transformation not only is possible but has always been the way change happens. Transformation, even on a large scale, has a personal dimension, and each individual matters. We believe such transformation involves a fundamental shift in our thinking, and an understanding and embodiment of collective wisdom.

We believe our capacity for collective wisdom is innate and its emergence in groups catalyzed by awareness of a compelling need and a higher purpose. The global crises we face, ranging from economic instability to resource sustainability, are each day encroaching more on our personal lives. There is a clear rationale for collective action. We see the beginnings of a social movement, grounded in wisdom, percolating up through social networks in the business world, nonprofit organizations, government agencies, and cross-cultural affiliations. In every community and organization are those whose uncommon behaviors are empathic, collective in their orientation, and far-reaching in their vision. We already have the human resources necessary to make a difference. Amid the crises we face is also an opportunity for seeking fresh perspectives on a grand scale. This book provides a framework for that search and a name for that movement.

Mark Gerzon, a leading conflict resolution facilitator and leadership trainer, and the author of *Leading Through Conflict*, wrote to us, "Humanity is hungering for wisdom. That is the word I hear most: not *compassion*; not *love*; not *peace*; not *kindness*—but *wisdom*. The other words all have deep meaning and their own unique power. But wisdom is the one that seems to magnetize people across the broadest spectrum around the world. I found myself drawn to this word because it is a cross-cutting theme in so many of the very diverse settings in which I am traveling."[2]

DEFINING OUR TERMS: COLLECTIVE, WISDOM, AND THE TRAP OF FOLLY

The dictionary defines *collective* as denoting a number of persons or things considered as one group or whole, marked by connection or similarity among or with the members of a group. In general, we use the term to designate a larger wholeness that may not be visible to the individual. For example, in groups we may be hardly conscious of being part of a collective because we see the world through an individualistic orientation. It is sometimes only in extreme circumstances or crisis that we recognize just how critical it is for groups to form a joint identity or combine and coordinate their diverse elements, or to become united behind a common purpose.

More often than not, we have a tendency to treat everything as separate and divisible. We analyze organizational structure and break it down into departments and functions. We diagram workflow and break it down into processes. We evaluate people and break them down into skills or job classifications. In a hospital setting, people can become diagnostic categories or simply dysfunctioning organs, such as "the bad kidney in room 6." We are so used to breaking things down into parts and pieces that we forget to look for what binds us together.

We must learn to shift our perspective back to what makes people and groups whole, to find what connects us together as a family, an organization, a nation, a world. Yet to do so requires a special kind of awareness. Collectivity without vigilance can come at a great cost. The collective can rob us of our distinctiveness, force upon us conformity, and rally us to war against an "other" who is not seen as part of our designated group. The collective can easily become synonymous with mobs, groupthink, and the lowest common denominator of group consensus, sacrificing anything original or even relevant to the circumstances that need to be addressed. Our book recognizes this in the form of collective behavior that leads to folly.

We define *folly* as lacking good sense, prudence, and foresight, a continuum of behaviors ranging from personally foolish behavior to criminality, evil, and depravity on a mass scale. Folly lacks discernment of fundamental human values and is a refusal to accept existing reality or to foresee the inevitable consequences of its actions. The result of folly can be mildly disconcerting or reach a scale of utter destruction and tragedy. It is a trap that all groups may find themselves in at some time and, once they're caught, difficult to extricate themselves from. Our book presents folly as a potentiality of every group and often the consequence of two related yet opposing dynamics: One is the movement in groups toward polarization, and the other is the movement toward false or forced agreement among the members.

We offer an alternative that is both hopeful and grounded in our research of groups. We believe the alternative is the human potential for finding ways to constructively work together and pursue wise action. By wise action, we mean the ability to exercise sound judgment, demonstrate good sense, and reflect a depth of understanding about people and situations. Wisdom in groups is demonstrated by insight, clarity, objectivity, and discernment rooted in deep caring and compassion.

By definition, wisdom is associated with accumulated philosophic or scientific learning but is distinguished by qualities of reverence and respect for life. *Wisdom*, as we use the term in this book, reminds us that we are part of something greater than ourselves alone. At a personal and group level, we link wisdom with thoughtfulness, an ability to reflect deeply on personal experience, and a capacity for applying discretion and intuitive understanding. Wisdom is a form of knowledge marked by our ability to discern the inner qualities and relationships of a situation. Considerate of multiple perspectives and forms of intelligence, wisdom often shows up in flashes of insight and new ways of understanding a situation. In groups, this can come in the form of *emergence*, something original or unexpected that moves the whole group forward or ties together disparate aspects of a situation.

When we join together the terms *collective* and *wisdom*, we reach a whole new synthesis of insight and revelation. Like binocular vision, in which both eyes are used at once, joining collective with wisdom is a way of seeing with added dimension and depth. The collective eye can pick up patterns of order, variation, and connections; wisdom can detect meaning and human values that arise spontaneously from a particular situation. We achieve, to paraphrase the words of the psychiatrist Viktor Frankl, an ability to weave together the slender threads of a fractured whole into a firmer pattern of meaning. To share collective wisdom with others is to make meaning from disparate threads and weave together a fresh understanding.

THE POWER OF COLLECTIVE WISDOM

So why should collective wisdom matter to us personally? Real change comes from an awareness of our deep connectedness. For some, this may mean a spiritual awakening, a transformation that begins with the human heart. For others, it may be a more intellectual process, coming to see anew the need for addressing an emerging environmental ethic and related social issues involving business, health, education, and the disparity of wealth within and between nations. However we come to this new awareness, the promise of wisdom offers something unique that is often absent from more traditional approaches to innovation, change, and progressive ideas. Wisdom offers greater meaning regarding the value of life for oneself and others. Wisdom teachings invariably draw our attention back to the indivisibility of the whole and the immediacy of the moment.

At the collective level, wisdom holds the key to redefining communities in the service of alternative futures that are life giving and sustainable. Collective wisdom invites us to think about the necessity of networks of people operating at the grassroots level to improve, invent, and discover new ways of enacting positive results. The outcome of a collective process that is wise is more likely a sound decision that goes beyond partisan concerns, and speaks instead to the aspirations of what is best in us and best for the circumstances at hand.

Collective wisdom helps us transcend the duality of self and others because it is a reminder that we are part of a larger framework from which we act out our role. As Shakespeare recognized, alone we are merely players, each with our exits and entrances, but as members of something larger, we become something extraordinary. "Consider," another wise poet said, "how the stars that shine more brightly manage to combine in constellations, get a name."[3] So too with collective wisdom: When we are in service to that which is life affirming and needed, we become something greater in combination with others.

The power of collective wisdom is to elicit new perspectives that reflect our common humanity and heal the divisions that keep us separated. Our ability to contribute to a better world, locally and globally, is magnified when we do it effectively with others. Similarly, dysfunction and divisions limit our contribution and lead us collectively into paralysis and negativity. Groups can be avenues for wisdom or unwittingly fall into traps of collective folly that foster false agreement and destructive polarities. The contribution of this book is to help readers navigate change that is alert to the potential of both wisdom and folly.

THIS BOOK AT A GLANCE

When human beings gather in groups or in communities, a depth of awareness and insight, a type of transcendent knowing, becomes available to us that can inform wise action and extraordinary results. We call this type of knowing *collective wisdom* and believe it to be a potential of *all* groups as an innate human capacity.

In chapter 1, we discuss what collective wisdom is and the qualities associated with the experience. Collective wisdom, as the phrase suggests, is not of the individual alone or purely an insight of the intellect or mind. Sometimes spontaneous in groups, sometimes the outcome of an extended period of time and attention, collective wisdom is a potential of all groups and is marked by an experience of deepening connections: within ourselves, with each other, and to larger natural forces involving nature, spirit, and our place in the cosmos.

While collective wisdom can have positive, even dramatic effects on our efforts in groups, we cannot will it to arise. The appearance of collective wisdom is unpredictable and often difficult to put into words, which reflects both its quality of immediacy and its deeper underlying purpose. The power of collective wisdom lies in its ability to be an emergent phenomenon—from uncertainty, inquiry, and dialogue come new meaning, learning, and unanticipated ways to move forward. Although we cannot will collective wisdom to arise in groups, we can make preparations that encourage it to emerge.

In chapter 2, we discuss six stances that can deepen our capacity for wise action and prepare us for collective wisdom to arise—illustrated with stories from diverse settings and times in history. We learn that we can increase the likelihood that collective wisdom will arise through the quality of how we listen and the conscious effort we make to suspend our personal certainty and seek diverse perspectives. We have the ability, personally and in groups, to read between the lines and listen with the wisdom of our heart.

In chapter 3, we explore these stances more fully by seeing how our internal perspective and external actions constitute a worldview. Through reflection on how our reality is shaped, we become better able to see the contours of a new consciousness, one that is more likely to create a positive future with others. The root meaning of the word *wisdom* involves seeing truths hidden from the casual observer. We bring attention to alternative worldviews that suggest we may be part of a larger collective consciousness, and why.

Being alert to wisdom, however, includes a necessary vigilance. In chapters 4–6, we discuss the pitfalls of an opposing potential—*collective folly*. Collective folly is a trap that all groups find themselves in at times, existing on a continuum from misguided or foolish behaviors to large-scale acts of depravity. As with collective wisdom, we believe that collective folly is a potential of *all* groups and is amplified by group dynamics involving polarization and false agreement. Every day, human beings commit small acts of foolishness and injustice, as well as unspeakable acts of violence and cruelty, within our families, among our friends, and against groups of strangers small and large that we deem as "other." By being alert to the potential presence of collective folly, we become more adept at cultivating a group wisdom that is realistic and tangible—unleashing extraordinary potential for innovation and change.

In chapter 7, we tell stories of groups and their capacity for innovation and change that reveal the power of collective wisdom for healing, creativity, and conflict resolution. Collective wisdom occurs most reliably when group members feel both safe and challenged to find what is best in themselves and what is best in and for the group. From such a vantage point, it becomes possible to heal old and current divisions, to experience true belonging to a vital community, to act creatively, and to feel hope about the larger world. When groups come together like this, a new threshold of co-creative power is reached.

In chapter 8, we learn how to embody the power of collective wisdom in acts of mindfulness. We learn how to continually return to the immediacy of our circumstances, create safe spaces for inquiry, and cultivate our transformative powers in the context of groups. Mindfulness keeps our attention on the present moment even as we must learn to act strategically and from a long-term perspective. Sometimes mistaken simply for a way to solve problems, the power of collective wisdom is in its ability to alter the way we pay attention to what will help us solve problems together. It is an affirmation of the common humanity we share with others.

one

What Is Collective Wisdom and How Does It Show Up?

Central Washington University and Western Oregon University were playing each other for a spot in the NCAA Division playoffs in women's softball. Up to the plate stepped Western Oregon's Sara Tucholsky, their five-foot-two right fielder, with two runners on base in the second inning. On the second pitch, the light-hitting outfielder blasted the ball over the center field fence for an apparent home run. Looking up to see the ball clear the fence, she missed first base as she rounded toward second and had to stop abruptly to return and touch it. But something in her right knee gave way and she collapsed on the base path. "I was in a lot of pain," she reported later. "Our first-base coach was telling me I had to crawl back to first base. 'I can't touch you,' she said, 'or you'll be out. I can't help you.'" Sara crawled through the dirt in obvious agony as her teammates and spectators watched her.[1]

The Western Oregon coach rushed onto the field and conferred with the umpires. They were clear that a player could not be assisted by her own teammates and that she would be credited with a single but not a home run. The Western Oregon coach did not know what to do; this was a crucial game, and it was Sara's first home run in four years.

Then Mallory Holtman stepped in. She was Central Washington's star first baseman and the player that other teams feared most. She offered a simple solution. If Sara's own teammates could not help her round the bases, what if Central Washington players did? The umpires concluded that there were no rules against an opposing team assisting. Mallory and her shortstop picked up Sara and resumed the home run walk, pausing at each base to let her touch her uninjured foot to the bag. Mallory recalled that they were laughing when they reached second base and wondered how this would look to others. When they reached home, they found out. The entire Western Oregon team was in tears. "My whole team was crying," Sara recalled. "Everybody in the stands was crying. My coach was crying. It touched a lot of people."

Western Oregon won the game 4–2, but that is not what Mallory Holtman took away as her lesson. "In the end, it is not about winning and losing so much," she reflected. "It was about this girl. She hit it over the fence and was in pain and she deserved a home run. . . . This is a huge experience I will take away. We are not going to remember if we won or lost, we are going to remember this kind of stuff that shows the character of our team. It is the best group of girls I've played with. I came up with the idea, but any girl on the team would have done it."

Mallory Holtman is a fine human being. When the moment came for her to act, she did not hesitate. Nor did she wonder whether her teammates would hesitate. *It is the best group of girls I've played with.* Indeed, her impulse to help was not seen as separate from her teammates: *I came up with the idea, but any girl on the team would have done it.*

The story of Sara and the aid she received from Mallory and her teammates flew over the Internet. It was as if in a sea of distress, evidence of human kindness was news. Yet it was news not because it was beyond our imagination, though the details were unusual, but because it was a reminder of what is common and decent in all of us. Yes, many would have left Sara to fend for herself, rationalized that the rules dictated the outcome, and felt justified, even fortunate, in her turn of bad luck. But Mallory Holtman did not hesitate to help, and her team backed her up.

How can we awaken to a world more like that? We see the results of a world in which the urge to dominate is everywhere, and even conversations can be competitive battlegrounds for winning and losing. How can we be part of settings, and help create settings, where the company we keep is more in step with human kindness, more likely to give others consideration and a helping hand?

FOUNDATIONAL QUALITIES AND
CHARACTERISTICS OF COLLECTIVE WISDOM

Collective wisdom is about how we come to make sound judgments with others, touched by what is common and decent in all of us. It is an insight or action recognizing that what happens to one happens to all. As such, it is not solely an analytic decision, a compromise, a vote, or even a win-win situation. Mallory knew enough about herself and enough about her teammates to act with a high degree of empathy that extended beyond her own group. This was no small feat regardless of its simplicity or the seemingly minor consequences at stake. *She hit it over the fence and was in pain and she deserved a home run* is a statement that has metaphoric power. We are capable of treating others, even those outside our own group, as we would want to be treated. We are capable of recognizing pain in others and responding to them. More often than we realize, we are adept at acting in the immediacy of the moment when something of real importance and value is at stake. These are characteristics that extend beyond the individual to groups, and they have real significance.

"I've been collecting stories about collective wisdom," cross-cultural anthropologist Angeles Arrien told us. "One was in Montana, where a Jewish family had a menorah in the window, and their home got completely trashed. The next morning, word got out, and by that evening, all the people in that community put a menorah in their window. That's an example of stopping violence in a collective, a unification that stopped violence."[2] It's the same message that Mallory Holtman conveyed in her actions with her team, but now set up in reverse: If it's done to one, it'll have to be done to all. Mallory Holtman saw beyond two separate teams, and the townspeople in Montana saw beyond two separate religions, both recognizing the larger humanity in which we are joined.

Reduced to its essence, collective wisdom evokes experiences of connection—an understanding that arises with others of right action and on behalf of a larger purpose. It is a form of knowledge that is not solely intellectual or based entirely on the knowledge of one person. This is what makes wisdom collective, though individuals often play a major part in collective wisdom's occurrence.

Collective wisdom is reflected in group behaviors that show human decency, social justice, and spiritual awareness. The effects of such behaviors result in surprising and positive outcomes that often cannot be ascribed to a simple or singular cause. Sometimes quite ordinary, other times quite profound, collective wisdom is what can happen when people find themselves in situations that invite new perspectives and evoke higher aspirations. Often, its emergence is grounded in a different way of listening and bringing attention to the immediacy of the moment.

A Silence on the River

I WAS IN A GROUP of about fifty people preparing to take our rafts into the water. There was a guide, a park ranger, who was Native American. His name was Vincent. We mostly didn't know each other. There was a lot of nervous energy in the group. People were chatting, checking their gear, eating. Some were expecting Vincent to speak and get the trip going. He didn't seem to be in a hurry. He sat quietly as the group bustled about. Finally, as the group energy settled, he began to talk. I don't remember him going through a long list of dos and don'ts about rafting, though I'm sure he shared with us the essentials of what we needed to know. What I remember instead was that he shared a bit about himself and why he worked as a ranger. He talked about the land we were on, and how his ancestors once lived here. He mentioned that there were times when he sat by himself that he could feel the presence of his ancestors still, and hear their voices in the wind and on the river.

When he finished, there was a noticeable calm that came over the group, and we began moving into the water, almost silently. It was really quite beautiful, as if we too might hear something in the sounds of the water and the wind.[3]

One of the essential qualities of collective wisdom is a palpable sense of connection with each other and to larger forces that is found, for example, in nature, in relationship to our ancestors, and even in relation to a physical place. Often these experiences are grounded in group members' understanding of the sacred, however defined by the individuals and the group. Carol Frenier, an author and an active participant in the Collective Wisdom Initiative, was interviewed by Craig Hamilton several years ago for an article about the growing interest in this phenomenon. During her interview, Frenier observed: "In these group experiences, people have access to a kind of knowing that's bigger than what we normally experience with each other. . . . You feel the presence of the sacred, and you sense that everybody else in the group is also feeling that."[4]

People who talk about their experiences of collective wisdom often report a sense of openness and awareness of something larger than themselves. The ability to communicate seems broader, and people are often astounded by the creativity that comes forward. "You have a sense," Frenier observed, "that the whole group is creating together, and you don't quite exactly know how."

This experience of connection, when it arises, often expands or dissipates our experience of boundaries—boundaries between different parts of ourselves, between ourselves and other members of the group, between our group and others outside of the group, between what is personal and what is universal. In a second interview conducted by Hamilton, a woman observed: "In the group, I experienced a kind of consciousness that was almost a singularity, like a dropping of personalities and a joining together where there was no sense of conflict. Nobody was in opposition and everybody was just helping each other. It became obvious that we weren't responding to individual personalities but were responding to something much deeper, much more real in each other that was collective, something that we shared—a commonality, really."[5]

Such experiences of connection, when they arise, can feel mystical, almost magical. But they are also quite *natural*. Certain kinds of conversations and collective endeavors, our colleague Meg Wheatley has written, take us to

> the wisdom we possess [in groups] that is unavailable to us as individuals. The wisdom emerges as we get more and more connected with each other, as we move from conversation to conversation, carrying the ideas from one conversation to another, looking for patterns, suddenly surprised by an insight we all share.
>
> There's a good scientific explanation for this, because this is how all life works. As separate ideas or entities become connected to each other, life surprises us with emergence—the sudden appearance of new capacity and intelligence. All living systems work in this way. We humans got confused and lost sight of this remarkable process by which individual actions, when connected, lead to much greater capacity.
>
> To those of us raised in a linear world with our minds shrunken by detailed analysis, the sudden appearance of collective wisdom always feels magical.[6]

Wheatley's last point may seem surprising: The emergence of collective wisdom can feel magical—somehow extraordinary or even unreal—because we have become so focused on the rational ("our minds shrunken by detailed analysis") that we have lost touch with other ways in which new capacity and intelligence come into being. Sometimes conversations and writings about collective wisdom can, perhaps unintentionally, reinforce this perception of the extraordinary nature of the phenomenon, intimating that collective wisdom is available only to the initiated. This is not our view. We maintain that collective wisdom is a potentiality of *all* groups, not just of so-called healthy or enlightened ones. This premise is not some declaration of naïve faith or a wistful prayer; we believe that collective wisdom is a potentiality of all groups because, as Wheatley writes, this is how *all* life works. New capacity and intelligence emerges through connections: from cell to cell, dendrite to dendrite, human to human, group to group. As extraordinary and mysterious as the experience of profound connection—and of collective wisdom emerging—may feel in the moment, collective wisdom as a phenomenon is natural, even potentially ordinary.

This does not mean that collective wisdom will emerge in every group, only that it can, whether the group is a women's softball team, a rural town, a one-time rafting expedition, a shared moment of profound awareness—or a team of hard-edged engineers and consultants confronting concrete challenges of sustainability. Peter Senge, who is often identified with the lessons that living systems have for organizational life, offered a story to us about this last kind of group as an example of boundaries expanding and dissipating, of deeper connections emerging.

For the Sake of Our Children

THE SOCIETY FOR ORGANIZATIONAL LEARNING has organized a Sustainability Consortium, a group of diverse people, including researchers, consultants, and executives from companies, who are embracing environmental and social sustainability as a cornerstone of their business strategy. This consortium works together through diverse action projects; its members meet together about twice a year.

One of the theories the consortium has explored was developed by John Ehrenfeld, director of the MIT Program on Technology, Business, and Environment. Ehrenfeld posits that building sustainable enterprises will require embracing three often-competing perspectives: the rationalistic, the naturalistic, and the humanistic. Some years ago, consortium members had a firsthand experience of the convergence of these three perspectives.

Xerox was hosting the meeting, and throughout the first day, members learned about Xerox's corporate philosophy of design for remanufacture. The company accounts for at least $250 million in cost savings due to remanufacture and waste reduction, a compelling illustration of the rationalistic perspective.

The group also toured the Document System 265 assembly area and saw firsthand what a "Zero to Landfill" work environment looks like. The production facility mimics nature by creating no waste—a powerful realization of the naturalistic perspective.

But at the end of the first day of meetings, the role of the humanistic perspective in Xerox's change effort was still only implicit. It was late in the afternoon, and consortium members were packed into a noisy, stuffy meeting room adjacent to the Document System 265 assembly area.

A young woman, one of the lead designers on the Xerox team, was talking about how meaningful it had been for her to be part of such an innovative effort when she was interrupted with an unusual question. A Consortium member from Ford, a veteran of many organizational learning projects, asked, "Helen, I understand what a great opportunity this was, and how exciting it was for you. I work with engineers and I know the intellectual excitement of pushing the technological envelope. But what I really want to know is: *Why* did you do this? What I mean is, what was the stand you took and *who were you* taking that stand?"

Helen looked at him for a long time in silence, and then, in front of many peers and a few superiors, she began to cry. "I am a mom," she said.

We all knew the team's motto, "Zero to landfill . . . for the sake of our children." But now we were in its presence. I suspect many of us will never forget the deep silence that filled the room. Another consortium member, a vice president from Ford/Visteon, turned to me and whispered, "seamlessness."[7]

In the story that Senge tells, a unifying element pulled together the different strands of the rational, naturalistic, and humanistic domains. There was a rational utilitarian benefit from remanufacture and waste reduction. There was the marvel of engineering skills that can mimic nature by creating no waste. There was a designer who was personally fulfilled by the challenge and possibilities of this effort. Yet, beyond these elements, there was something additional, something unexpected: a question that lifted the group to another level. It was a very personal question that elicited a very personal answer. "I am a mom," she answered, and her eyes welled up with tears. She did this in front of her peers and supervisors. There was risk involved. She was at once exquisitely vulnerable and quietly beautiful in her honesty. It had the effect of deepening the silence that began when she listened to the question and took it seriously, pausing to find within herself the most direct answer.

With Helen's answer, there was a convergence of varied perspectives. The company's motto—*Zero to landfill . . . for the sake of our children*—stopped for a moment being just a motto and became something real and alive. It was a memorable moment, one that Senge felt was unlikely to be forgotten. This is common in our conversations with people about such moments—there is something vital, something that just feels so alive that it wants to burst out on its own. Seamlessness. An experience of a larger whole emerging as boundaries expand and connections grow stronger: within an individual group member, within a project team, within a business model, within an industry, within a world.

Collective wisdom is often revealed as people and worldviews mix and collide, sometimes beautifully as in Senge's tale, and sometimes with turbulence. Often, a catalytic moment—in this case, the question and response that expressed authenticity and vulnerability—moves the group into a new space or territory of understanding. In spiritual traditions, such as Zen Buddhism, this might be understood as a shift away from duality, erasing the concreteness of something having to be true or not true and moving instead toward a larger truth inclusive of multiple perspectives. However we might want to understand it, the higher aspiration that was indicated by the simple statement "I am a mom" drew into focus the richness of the group's collective efforts and the meaning for a better life that the higher aspiration held for them and others.

BEYOND THE INTELLECT, BEYOND THE INDIVIDUAL

While some writers speak of collective intelligence, we use the term collective wisdom to reflect a quality of group understanding that is neither of the intellect alone nor of any individual alone. When this knowing and sense of right action emerges, it does so from deep within the individual participants, from within the collective awareness of the group, and from within the larger field of spiritual, cultural, and institutional forces that surround any group activity.

Many people who describe experiences of collective wisdom describe a physicality to the experience, a feeling of discernment in their personal body and an awareness of permeability with others. In another interview by Craig Hamilton, a woman said this of her group experience: "When someone else spoke, it felt as if I was speaking. And when I did speak, it was almost egoless, like it wasn't really me. It was as if something larger than me was speaking through me. The atmosphere in the room felt like we were in a river. . . . We started to say things that we had never thought before . . . something would be revealed, and that would open up something else to be revealed."[8]

Sometimes this quality of understanding can manifest in a sudden and shared sense of what to do next, a knowing that extends beyond words and amplifies a shared sense of connection and purpose with others. Often, this knowing can emerge from uncertainty, a "not knowing" that requires added personal reflection and listening to divergent perspectives. We become less "expert" but more open. The cognitive scientist Francisco Varela explains how this can be true because at the "moments of breakdown, that is, when we are *not* experts . . . we become like beginners seeking to feel at ease with the task at hand."[9] In other words, it is at just those moments when our world is less familiar to us that we have the chance to see in new ways and embody new actions.

One of the paradoxes of collective wisdom is that such insights are far more likely to arise when the group is willing to risk, or admit, not knowing. Juanita Brown recalls this moment experienced by a group that reached a point of surrender to not knowing.

I Don't Know, but Maybe We Do

THE YEAR IS 1966. THE grape fields of California are ablaze with conflict and tension. Cesar Chavez and his fledgling United Farm Workers are seeking negotiations through collective bargaining elections with the DiGiorgio Corporation—the largest grower of table grapes in the nation. Many new workers are frightened, already indentured by the company who paid their way from Mexico and now living in DiGiorgio's labor camps. They support their brothers and sisters in the United Farm Workers who are seeking a better life, but they have children to feed and no passage home.

The farm labor camps, row on row of cinder block housing, are located on company property. There are watchtowers overlooking the camps, silent reminders of earlier days when the Japanese were interned in these same buildings during World War II. There are no longer guards in the towers but there are guards at the gates. Because the camps are on private property, United Farm Worker organizers have been barred from entry—barred from engaging in conversations with the workers inside—barred from discussing the workers' democratic rights under the law to vote for the United Farm Workers to represent them in conversations with the growers. A paradox—workers have the right to vote in the first election in agricultural history but not the means to share in the conversation needed to make an informed choice on behalf of a better life for themselves and their families.

What to do? Cesar Chavez and farm worker organizers are on the roadside at 5 AM as the trucks leave for the fields, passing small informational leaflets through the slats of the trucks. The growers have permitted informational leafleting.

Even Cesar is beginning to lose hope. He calls a meeting of the whole community. Men, women, children: the farm worker meeting hall is full. The mood is somber. Cesar explains the situation to those gathered, realistically, honestly, without artifice.

Cesar says he has no answer to the dilemma. If there is no way to engage in conversation with the workers in the camps, it will be hard to change our future, he says. He asks for their honest assessment, for ideas, for help. All bearing witness know that some unforeseen breakthrough is the only way through.

People share ideas, many ideas. None are rejected. Everyone is asked not to debate because no decision is going to be made tonight. We are trying to listen, he says, listen to every voice that wants to be heard.

Many voices enter the conversation. The meeting is nearly done. Way in the back of the hall sits an old woman wrapped in a rebozo, a Mexican shawl. She stands and speaks quietly in Spanish.

"Well, I know I am not qualified, but there was something . . . I had an idea, maybe just a small idea, but maybe it can help. If we can't go in to visit the workers, maybe there is a way they could come to us. I believe only God can help us now. Why don't we build an altar, a small church on the public road-way across the street from the camps? We can hold Mass and a prayer vigil every night. I know there are priests who will help us. The workers can come across the street to the Mass and the prayer vigil. The growers can't stop them from coming to a prayer vigil, can they? And they can't stop us from holding one, can they? And as we pray together with the workers from the camps, they will come to know who we are and what we stand for and then they can vote in a better way for their future. . . ."

As the person who translated the old woman's words from Spanish, I think somehow the energy of her presence, the power of her simplicity, and the sigh of *Yes* that emerged from the collective in the room will remain forever etched in my own being.[10]

What is this community struggling for? For the right to have conversations, for the right to gather with farm workers and engage them in dialogue about how the United Farm Workers might help them. The mood is somber; everyone knows what's at stake. The UFW is a fledgling organization in 1966. It has just recently launched the grape boycott. A setback in these fields would be devastating not only for the workers here but for the larger movement as well.

Cesar Chavez calls the group together, not to ratify a plan he has already developed, but to confess that he does not know what to do. No one else does, either. So they gather: not to debate, not even to decide, but to listen to "every voice that wants to be heard." Everyone is needed because no one individual, not even the leader, has the answer. Many people speak; none are rejected. And then, from the back of the room, an old woman who wonders if she is even qualified risks sharing an idea. She changes the very nature of the question: If we can't go to them, can we invite them to us? In a place of past and present imprisonment, can we extend an invitation that allows them freedom to choose? For Juanita Brown, the energy of this woman's presence and the simplicity of her profound questions shifted the trajectory in the room. Suddenly, there was a way forward. Yes. *The sigh of Yes that emerged . . . will remain forever etched in my own being.*

How is this possible? How does it happen that from a place of not knowing, of even hopelessness, a way forward emerges? A first response might be to appreciate the mystery of collective wisdom's emergence. An additional response, however, might point to what becomes possible when we authentically confess to not knowing. In such moments of surrender, we may open to a knowing that transcends the intellect alone, a knowing that is beyond any one of us, a knowing that may not have been possible when the certainty of the mind crowded all else out. The "small idea" put forward by the old woman seeded new possibilities; she is the set breaker, in systems language. As with Mallory Holtman's role in the opening story, a certain logic that shackled the group was released. If we cannot gain access by pushing our way in, would it be possible to draw people out? The group is "lifted up" by the possibilities of a new approach.

PERCEPTIBLE, POSITIVE, OFTEN SURPRISING EFFECTS

So what happened after the community meeting? A day or so later, the group parked Chavez's old station wagon across the road from the camp gates and erected a small altar in the back. At first, only a few workers came, then many, and then many more. When the election was held, the workers voted to have the UFW represent them.

Collective wisdom is a transformative shift that affects both inner awareness and outer behavior. These effects can benefit individuals within the group; the whole group; and individuals, groups, and larger collectives impacted by the group's work. They are also positive to the extent that they serve the larger social impulses for wholeness, fairness, compassion, and justice.

Sometimes the shifts are dramatic, as in the election that certified the UFW to represent the DiGiorgio workers. Sometimes they are subtle, as in the designer's ability to embody a collective vision of "Zero to landfill—for the sake of our children." Sometimes they are subtler still, as members began to move in concert and support each other as they embarked on a rafting trip.

Collective wisdom emerges when people open to it and don't try to control and will it into being, so its effects are frequently surprising and in some cases unimaginable before they unfold. We doubt that anyone went into the UFW community meeting thinking, "I know: an altar on the back of a Chevy!" The effects are surprising because they are not predetermined; they arise through the connections and conversations that unfold within the group. Wisdom arises in the gaps between what is known and unknown, in the small openings that allow new meanings and perspectives to take hold.

SUMMARY: SOUND JUDGMENT AND REVELATION

Collective wisdom is about the nature of sound judgments made with others, reflecting a deep understanding of people and situations. It often involves an insight or revelation that what happens to one happens to all. Accordingly, we feel an instinct for ethical and constructive action in the moment. Collective wisdom shows up in our ways of being together— sometimes experienced as sacredness; or being part of a flow state; or feeling an expansion and dissipation of boundaries with others, nature, and spirit.

Throughout this chapter, we have also pointed to some of the paradoxes of collective wisdom. It is a mystery that has predictable patterns. It is an understanding beyond the intellect; it is a knowing that emerges from not knowing. The experience of collective wisdom can be extraordinary, and it is natural, even common, in groups. Collective wisdom depends on conversation and is most powerfully felt in the silences that arise within those conversations. Collective wisdom is experienced in groups, yet it is often catalyzed by or reflected in the behavior of an individual. Finally, collective wisdom has positive, even dramatic effects on group cohesion and action, yet it cannot be willed into existence, controlled, or even planned for. What can we do to bring it forth?

We believe we can prepare for it and increase the likelihood that it will emerge. The commitments and convictions instrumental for preparation are the focus of our next chapter.

two

Preparing for Collective
Wisdom to Arise

Our colleague Kate Regan uses a simple exercise to prepare individuals in groups to notice their internal
thoughts and calibrate their group behaviors. In this exercise, typically done in workshops of approximately twenty
people who are seated in a circle, she asks the participants
to look down at the floor and close their eyes. She tells
them that without opening their eyes, they must count to
thirty in sequence without two people speaking at the same
time. If two people do speak simultaneously, they must
begin again. As you might expect, rarely do groups accomplish this the first time. As they report later, many individuals develop strategies to get the task done quickly without

any sense of knowing what others are doing. For example, one person may decide to call out a number immediately once the exercise begins, or another may decide to call out his number at the split second after another person finishes. They learn that these individual strategies collide with each other, and two or three people inevitably call out at the same time.

Remarkably, most groups end up succeeding at the task, but only after there is a shift in their attitude and behavior. What happens is that participants suspend their individual strategies and begin to sense into the rhythm of the group. This requires a different set of skills and competence than an approach that is solely individual or analytic. It is more like a jazz musician sensing the openings and transitions in the flow of the music. Rather than the punctuated sounds of individuals' punching out their numbers, a noticeable quiet settles over the group. Individuals begin to sense a different energy in the room and pay attention to a different part of themselves. In the language of collective wisdom, they sense what is arising among them in the immediacy of the moment. How can we do more of this? How can we increase this kind of competence and attentiveness in ourselves as well as groups?

So far we have described what collective wisdom is and some of the key qualities associated with the experience. Now we will look at stances, found through our research and experience, that can increase the likelihood of collective wisdom emerging. A *stance* is an attitude and bearing involving commitment and conviction. These are choices of internal perspective and external action that we make in the day-to-day and moment-by-moment interactions we have with others. Such a stance can be learned and practiced, becoming a new way of being in relationship with others, a new type of human association leading to unleashing the spirit of cooperation and unlimited cocreation in groups. The stances are as follows:

DEEP LISTENING

Collective wisdom begins with a commitment to recognize that we are more than just the sum of our external parts. There is an interior realm within individuals, groups, and larger collectives. Deep listening invites us to be curious about what is *really* going on inside the person, the group, or the larger collective. It is an act of being fully present with others, not simply an act of hearing or memory. What do people really feel, dream, and fear? Deep listening is a way to pay attention to both interior and exterior worlds in order for groups to make sounder judgments and act in accordance with deeper values.

SUSPENSION OF CERTAINTY

A transcendent discovery is far more possible for individuals and groups when there is a willingness to risk, or admit, not knowing—when we confront directly the full weight of our confusion or the dilemma we are facing. The human capacity to make meaning together depends on a suspension of any one individual or subgroup's having always to be in the right. This commitment to suspend certainty is what makes our *knowing together* collective, because something new and often unexpected emerges in and through the group. A greater collective wisdom becomes possible because ideas are no longer the possession of one person or subgroup, but are shared by those who helped shape it together. A suspension of certainty is akin to beginner's mind, a commitment to *not know* in order for new knowledge to arise.

SEEING WHOLE SYSTEMS/SEEKING DIVERSE PERSPECTIVES

This stance shifts our attention from the individual to the group. Each group member sees the world in a unique way, but all the information is valuable and part of the whole. Our diverse perspectives, therefore, matter because they reveal more of the whole system. This is why groups need to gather information from many perspectives: to increase their understanding of the whole. Committing to this stance requires us to find ways to synthesize diverse information, whether through multiple personal conversations, through data collection, or through group methodologies that emphasize listening and discovery.

RESPECT FOR OTHERS/GROUP DISCERNMENT

Respect is a commitment to esteem others, even when disagreements arise. It is a willingness to recognize dissent as an avenue for new learning. Discernment is a capacity in groups for differentiation, permitting the emergence of new thinking and new images of what is possible. When respect and discernment are brought together, groups have a renewed ability to find common ground—even when such a direction seems difficult or obstructed. This commitment creates the conditions for alignment of personal, group, and higher-order values such as justice, compassion, and freedom. Although never perfect, this stance allows for the development of productive relationships and directed action in accord with a common purpose.

WELCOMING ALL THAT IS ARISING

How we invite others into relationship matters. The stance of welcoming brings conscious attention to how gracefully we treat each other—recognizing different needs, respecting differences, and celebrating our common humanity. It brings attention to sharing power with others and treating others as equals. This commitment also encourages us to welcome the pleasant and unpleasant aspects of group life, recognizing that even disruptive obstacles or difficult circumstances can be critical aspects of our passage to wholeness.

TRUST IN THE TRANSCENDENT

Underlying and critical to all the stances that aid collective wisdom's emergence is a respect for human agency, the powers of nature, and the significance of a spiritual dimension to the activities we undertake. When we look out upon the world with awe and wonder, we are better able to see constructive possibilities rather than simply constricting limits. There is a Chinese expression that says when we step back, we can see more of the ocean and sky. Trust in the transcendent is the invitation to see a larger natural world on which the human journey is written. We become capable of remaining secure even in our uncertainty and better able to ask others for assistance, cocreating a world that works for all.

To illustrate how a stance for collective wisdom can be embodied and lived, we offer four stories from four key thought leaders and practitioners in the field of collective wisdom: Paula Underwood, Jacob Needleman, Lauren Artress, and Jerry Sternin. We have chosen these stories for their diversity and their ability to reveal examples of actions and beliefs that aid collective wisdom's emergence.

DEEP LISTENING, RESPECT FOR OTHERS/ GROUP DISCERNMENT

How does one cultivate an orientation of *deep listening*? How can we listen to what is said "between the words" as much as to the content of the words themselves? What is a way to respect "all the voices in the room" when it is not always possible to be physically present together in the same room?

We had a chance to talk with Paula Underwood, a member of the Turtle clan of the first five nations of the Iroquois. Author of *The Walking People: A Native American Oral History*, she was a Keeper of the ancient traditions handed down to her from an agreement made by her great-great-grandmother two hundred years ago to keep alive the wisdom of her people. Her teaching and consulting work in systems and cross-cultural understanding has touched the lives of elementary-school children, graduate students, and corporate executives.

Underwood addressed with us an approach to consensus that is often confused with getting "agreement" simply for the sake of pacifying certain members or to avoid conflict.

Her description of *one mind* amplifies those qualities of collective wisdom that point to a knowing that emerges through our internal senses and empathic connection with others. She speaks of allowing answers to emerge from a relational field grounded in respect and compassion. Deep listening, as she describes it, prepares the ground for collective wisdom to emerge, and she offers a very personal story of how she learned this for herself. Her words open for us a window on the inner workings of an indigenous community where roles and relationships are integrated to further the spirit of group cohesion.

May We Be of One Mind

From an interview with Paula Underwood,
clan mother of the Turtle clan, Iroquois nation[1]

Paula Underwood:

AS FAR AS I KNOW, almost all the people, on the northern part of Turtle Island at least, made their decisions on the basis of group consensus. And that doesn't mean that everybody gets in a circle and all nine thousand people speak up. It does mean that you begin a process of learning to understand the members of your group in such a way that you can project reasonably well what their views will be on a given issue. So the general understanding always rises from the people.

The specific application then can safely be made by counselors based on that general understanding. In Iroquois terms, you'd say, "May we be of one mind." You don't have agreement until you are of one mind.

You've probably heard that every decision must be made on the basis of what the impact will be in the seventh generation ahead.

Leaders are responsible to feed the mind and the spirit of the people, and you feed the mind with good information.

Well, just as the clan mothers are responsible to count the ears of corn and to make sure there is enough to see us through the winter and indeed through the next three winters in case the crop is bad next year, so the clan mothers are responsible to feed the mind and spirit.

You are chosen as a clan mother for your ability to know the people's heart. So a clan mother is somebody who knows how to listen. And she knows how to listen whether anyone's saying something or not, if you see what I mean.

How does one learn that?

When I was a little bitty kiddy, about five, my dad began a process . . . anytime somebody came and said something to us, my dad would say, "You remember what he said, honey girl?"

And I would tell my father what the person said until I got so good at it that I could repeat verbatim even long presentations of what the person had said. And he did this all the time.

And finally one day there was this old gentleman, Richard Thompson. I still remember his name; he lived across the street. And every time my dad started to mow the lawn, here comes Mr. Thompson. And so I would stand out there.

Dad says, "You might come and listen to this man, honey girl. He's pretty interesting." And so I listened to him, and then my dad would say, "What did you hear him say?" And I would tell him.

Well, eventually I was repeating all the stories he liked to share with my dad verbatim. I knew them all by heart.

And my dad says, "You're getting pretty good at that. *Did you hear his heart?*" And I thought, what?

So I went around for days with my ear to people's chests trying *to hear their hearts.*

Finally my dad created another learning situation for me by asking my mother to read an article from the newspaper.

He says, "Well, I guess if you want to understand that article, you have to read between the lines."

I thought, oh, read between the lines. Hear between the words. And the next time I listened to Mr. Thompson's stories, I tried to listen between the words.

And my dad said, "I know you know his story. Did you hear his heart?" And I said, yes. He is very lonely and comes and shares his memories with you again and again because he's asking you to keep him company in his memories. And it just came out of me. In other words, my heart echoed his heart. And when you can listen at that level, then you can hear not only the people. If you really pay attention, you can hear what the Universe is saying.

COMMENTARY

Paula Underwood's words highlight three kinds of preparation that create the conditions for collective wisdom's emergence. First is looking forward in time. Making decisions on the basis of their impact seven generations forward obligates us to value the future in the present moment and consider the consequences of our actions over time. In a practical sense, it means that group members can anticipate the future together before it happens, even considering unintended consequences that might result from specific decisions. It also means simultaneously having shorter time frames (such as three winters) to prepare contingencies in case of difficult times. Underwood herself was a product of this commitment to look forward in time and to value what would be needed for future generations. She was the fifth generation of her family to be the Keeper of Iroquois traditions and to tell their story of ten thousand years, an account that in her words was not a "catalog of kings. It is instead a history of a people learning together."

The second form of preparation is a demonstration of how empathy and compassion support the unity of the group as a whole. Empathy asks that we see, at least for a moment, through someone else's eyes. Compassion asks that we recognize human frailty and suffering, and share with others our loving attention. These are capacities we develop within ourselves through a gradual process of learning and maturation. They are also capacities that develop a group's readiness for deepening insight and directed action. In Underwood's interview, she communicated to us the responsibility of people in leadership roles to provide good information, but also of everyone to become more skillfully attentive to "reading between the lines" and listening to each other's hearts.

The third form of preparation is implied by the way she talked with us—her use of story, symbol, metaphor, and repetition to emphasize her points and evoke an understanding of her true intent. At one point in the interview, she described this as a way of communicating that is "using your sense of wholeness, as well as your sequential logic. You're combining the two, which is something my tradition always tries to do, and these days we say you're using both left and right brain. And that's really critical. You have to get both functioning." Preparing for collective wisdom's emergence requires us as individuals and in groups to use both our logical and symbol-making minds. "Symbols," Underwood told us, "are in effect a door through which you can walk to the greater understanding." We need to make room in groups for this kind of more sophisticated understanding, incorporating sequential logic and spontaneous insights, linear progressions and intuitive leaps, bullet points and poetry. Collective wisdom is more likely to arise when sound judgment is based on the entirety of our multiple intelligences.

TRUST IN THE TRANSCENDENT AND THE SUSPENSION OF CERTAINTY

Jacob Needleman is one of our great modern philosophers and also one of the originating inspirations for the Collective Wisdom Initiative. Some ten years ago, in a letter to the president of the Fetzer Institute, the foundation that sponsored our research, he wrote of the pressing need for new social forms that would address the growing fragmentation and balkanization of our communities: "We obviously cannot confront this tangled world alone. . . . It takes no great insight to realize that we have no choice but to think together, ponder together, in groups and communities. The question is how to do this. How to come together and think and hear each other in order to touch, or be touched by, the intelligence we need." His answer suggested a depth of insight arising in groups from a confluence of forces, joining the inner spiritual life of the individual with the outer circumstances and conflicts that confront groups all the time. He wrote: "I [believe] that the group is the art form of the future. . . . In our present culture the main need is for a form that can enable human beings to share their perceptions and attention and, through that sharing, to become a conduit for the appearance of spiritual intelligence."[2]

Needleman was pointing to a form of intelligence we have heard described in our research on collective wisdom and that has been our own experience. He was suggesting that we can suspend our desire for individual certainty on behalf of a larger, more compelling and ultimately more inclusive vision. The group is the art form of this kind of human association.

At the time, he was working on his book *The American Soul: Rediscovering the Wisdom of the Founders*. In it, he articulated the historical antecedents of this group vision by studying the American founders' formulation of government and specifically democracy's transformative document—the Constitution of the United States of America. Drawing from his book and our conversations with him, here is our account of Jacob Needleman's retelling of the story of the Constitutional Convention, the role Benjamin Franklin played, and the larger implications for collective wisdom emerging.

The Creation of the
U.S. Constitution

*Based on conversations with Jacob Needleman
and on his book* The American Soul [3]

IN MOSTLY SWELTERING SUMMER HEAT, the Constitutional Convention took place in Philadelphia over almost four months in 1787. The windows were shuttered closed, and an agreement to maintain secrecy was kept throughout the proceedings. After a month of quarreling, bitterness, and contentious debate, there were ample reasons to believe that failure was a real possibility.

At the age of eighty-one and suffering from gout, Benjamin Franklin, a delegate to the convention, rose to speak to the group:

> The small progress we have made after four or five weeks' close attendance and continual reasonings with each other, our different sentiments on almost every question . . . is, methinks, a melancholy proof of the imperfection of human understanding.[4]

Franklin suggested to the group members that they were seeking wisdom in the wrong places—from the past or from political models in Europe. He called instead for them to become a conduit for spirit:

In this situation of this assembly, groping, as it were, in the dark to find political truth, and scarce able to distinguish it when presented to us, how has it happened, Sir, that we have not hitherto once thought of humbly applying to the Father of Lights to illuminate our understanding? . . . And have we now forgotten that powerful Friend? Or do we imagine we no longer need its assistance?[5]

"I picture Franklin reminding them," wrote Needleman, reflecting on whether Franklin's words had any impact on the delegates, "of what a man is willing to let go of when the need for a greater force in oneself is felt and understood. But I do not picture Franklin believing that his words are actually going to turn the tide and bring harmony to the delegation. He is too worldly wise to expect that." Needleman wonders if Franklin may indeed be holding up to the group a mirror of his own exhaustion, "that he is too ready to give up listening, too ready to let things go by power plays and egoism, the all too familiar forces of wishful thinking and paranoia."[6]

Needleman continues with his story:

The days, weeks and months passed by. The heat increased, the wrangling and quarreling went on, the danger of dissolution increased. How often it must have seemed that the colonies would break apart—that fear and mistrust and individual opinion would prevail, or that the final resolution would be a weak and ineffectual document that, in the absence of obvious external danger, would only hold the colonies together until the next crisis or the one after that blew them apart. How clear it probably would have seemed to an outside observer that no real depth of unity would ever be achieved by these men who in general sought not a deep and greater good for the whole, but only a greater good for their own interests....

And yet, a union was formed, a union beyond economic, military, legal, religious or political bonds, a union that has lasted amid forces that in the past two centuries have broken down every other government in the world. The Constitution of the United States has allowed the coherence of a people and a nation within whose geographical and psychological borders all the immense forces of human life on earth have played and clashed with intensity beyond any imagining.

What force lies at the origin of the Constitution of the United States, beyond what may be labeled economic, political, legal, military or religious influences in any of their obvious meanings? What enabled the Constitution as we know it to come into existence?

Is not the answer to this question to be found in the nearly superhuman struggle of individuals to listen to each other? If we are to discern a spiritual resonance in the founding of America, will it not be seen mainly in the effort of individuals to open their minds to each other when almost everything in them is pulling them into isolation? I do not say that all or even many of the delegates of the Constitutional Convention undertook soul-searching efforts, or that they listened to each other for the purpose of spiritual freedom. This group was not a collection of spiritual aspirants. Nevertheless, we can take the "miracle" of the formation of the Constitution as a great external sign of a process that can take place when individuals come together to seek understanding and right action. If government is the art form of America, if the Constitution is the masterpiece of this art, then there must lie within the process of its formation lessons that we shall need to learn.... *The art of the future is the group.* The intelligence and benevolence we need can only come from the group, from associations of men and women seeking to struggle against the impulses of illusion, egoism, and fear.[7]

Let us skip to the end of the convention. Needleman recounts the final movement in the symphony of actions, reactions, secret meetings, compromises, agreements, lapses of judgment, and self-interest that shaped the final document. Franklin himself, old and wise and respected by his colleagues, had been rebuffed in many of his key positions. He argued for and lost in his advocacy for proportional representation based on state population. Fearing corruption, he lost in his argument against salaries for the president and members of Congress. An abolitionist, he accepted that the issue of slavery would not be confronted, leaving a wounding that future generations would have to solve. How then to balance the distaste of parts while believing in the necessity of the whole?

On September 17, 1787, the last day of the Constitutional Convention, Franklin composed a speech that sought to rally those still on the fence regarding its signing. Franklin, whose formal education never went beyond penmanship, had taught himself to pay attention to style, organization, and insightfulness. Now, he was putting his lifetime learning together in a final argument for democracy. Franklin was too weak to give the speech himself, so it was read by James Wilson, a fellow Pennsylvanian.

Mr. President,

> I confess that I do not entirely approve of this Constitution
> at present; but, Sir, I am not sure I shall never approve it;
> for having lived long, I have experienced many instances
> of being obliged, by better information or fuller consider-
> ations, to change my opinions even on important subjects,
> which I once thought right, but found to be otherwise. It is
> therefore that, the older I grow, the more apt I am to doubt
> my own judgment of others.[8]

In his final words to the convention, Franklin chose to articulate the one quality that distinguished democracy from
past forms of government. This quality was citizens' ability
to reach beyond human fallibility and collective foolishness
to find wisdom together. To do this, however, required from
each of them a certain humility and suspension of certainty.
Franklin continued:

> Most men, indeed, as well as most sects in religion, think
> themselves in possession of all truth, and that wherever
> others differ from them, it is so far error. Steele, a Protestant,
> in a dedication, tells the Pope, that the only difference be-
> tween our two churches in their opinions of the certainty
> of their doctrine, is the Romish Church is *infallible*, and the
> Church of England is *never in the wrong*. But although many
> private persons think almost as highly of their own infallibil-
> ity as that of their sect, few express it so naturally as a cer-
> tain French Lady, who, in a little dispute with her sister, said,
> "But I meet with nobody but myself that is always in the
> right." *"Je ne trouve que moi qui aie toujours raison."*

In these sentiments, Sir, I agree to this Constitution, with all its faults—if they are such; because I think a general government necessary for us, and there is no form of government but what may be a blessing to the people, if well administered; and I believe, farther, that this is likely to be well administered for a course of years, and can only end in despotism, as other forms have done before it, when the people shall become so corrupted as to need despotic government, being incapable of any other.[9]

COMMENTARY

Franklin articulates with wit and alacrity of association the reason why suspension of certainty is needed—taking on the church in Rome and the Church of England with a twist of French arrogance thrown in. In just a few words, he is able to equate divine infallibility with the very human inclination to feel "always in the right." He asserts that infallibility is the mark of the past and the antithesis of what democracy requires. The group, he warns, is in jeopardy whenever one individual or one subgroup believes it must always have the right idea or single solution. His words function as a bridge taking us from past reliance on certainty to the threshold of a new kind of human association based on listening and cooperation—even under the most difficult challenges. This is the legacy we still celebrate to this day.

Through Needleman's eyes we see some of Franklin's ability to provoke new understanding and feel in Franklin's words his power to understand people and situations. He understands that government is a necessary but external structure that will thrive when well administered and wither when the collective is no longer capable of maintaining it. He sees how it is possible, through seeking to serve a greater aim, to consciously struggle with attachment to one's opinions—a quality Needleman calls the "metaphysics of democracy." He is able to elevate and reframe even the most petty of disagreements to its place in a larger conversation about the future of our collective efforts.

Democracy is a fragile agreement that depends on the art and power of the group and on our capacity to allow reason to enter us communally. Genuine democracy is the power that comes from listening each other into a new being, a collective being that is as conscious of its wholeness as of its differences. Franklin's words foreshadow the dialogic writings of the philosopher Martin Buber and the physicist David Bohm, who asserted, "Real dialogue is where two or more people become willing to suspend their certainty in each other's presence."

The power of collective wisdom issues forth from listening, beyond surface concerns, to the deeper well of wisdom that lies in each of us and among us. From this struggle to hear each other is the preparation for a transcendent understanding. It is a cultivation of what has genuine significance for each other and the group as a collective entity. It is a knowledge that joins the search for greater purpose with a spiritual intelligence that derives from humility. *And have we now forgotten that powerful Friend?* Franklin asked. *Or do we imagine we no longer need its assistance?* And it can grow from the most precarious and rocky of circumstances.

The story of the Constitutional Convention holds lessons for what is necessary to prepare for collective wisdom's emergence: an ability to listen beyond the partisan position or particular loyalties of the moment. Wisdom's emergence in groups depends on a delicate weaving back and forth between our ability to suspend personal certainty and our competence to hear a quiet voice from a source deep within us. Needleman's account reminds us of an actual event that holds symbolic significance:

> Between, or rather above, these two opposite poles—the sentimental and the cynical views of our history—there hovers the element of symbolic reality, of an actual process that took place in actual history which yet at the same time has about it the fragrance of a process that could lead all men and women toward the moral power and intelligence we are searching for. This kind of process took place during the blistering Philadelphia summer—the process of a group of ordinary human beings *listening* to each other, not as people usually listen, but as people *can* listen: from a source deeper in themselves which opens them not only to the thoughts and views of their neighbor, but to something wiser and finer in themselves and, perhaps, in the universe itself.[10]

"*Never forget that the true character of our nation is revealed not during times of comfort and ease, but by the right we do when the moment is hard. I ask you to help me reveal that character once more, and together, we can carry forward as one nation, and one people, the legacy of our forefathers that we celebrate today.*"

—Barack Obama, forty-fourth President of the United States, in a pre-inaugural address.[11]

WELCOMING ALL THAT IS ARISING

The willingness to suspend personal certainty on behalf of a greater collective benefit is something we can all learn to practice and embody. So too is the stance of *welcoming all that is arising*. The need to open to guidance from the unexpected and sometimes disturbing elements of group life distinguishes collective wisdom from many group processes. Intentionally or not, leaders often attempt to control or contain the unexpected elements of group life. Welcoming all that is arising suggests a capacity to accept, and even welcome, the sudden obstacle or seeming distraction. As with the stance of trusting in the transcendent, we are reminded to be open to the larger meaning that is possible for us when we step back from the discomfort of the moment. How we accomplish this depends on a certain level of inner preparation and conscious awareness that events are unfolding around us, whether we like it or not.

We had the opportunity to talk with Lauren Artress, Episcopal priest and founder and creative director of Veriditas, a nonprofit organization dedicated to introducing people to the healing, meditative powers of the labyrinth. The labyrinth is an ancient pattern found in many cultures around the world. Inscribed on pottery, tablets, and tiles that date as far back as five thousand years, the labyrinth design is based on spirals and circles mirrored in nature. In Native American tradition, the labyrinth has similarities to the Medicine Wheel; in mystical Judaism, the Kabala; in Celtic traditions, the never-ending circle. A feature common to labyrinths is that they have one path that winds circuitously to the center. The labyrinth represents a different way of seeing, a different kind of perception altogether—one that values and makes good use of symbolic meaning and metaphor.

Artress, who is the author of three books on the labyrinth and is identified with launching what is now known as the Labyrinth Movement, recounted to us the story of a quite unexpected and potentially disruptive experience. Her story sheds light on how the unplanned moment becomes preparation for deepening insight and collective awareness.

Encountering the Stranger

From an interview with Lauren Artress, founder and creative director of Veriditas [12]

Lauren Artress:

THIS IS A STORY ABOUT a time we were doing labyrinth work at a monastery in Pecos, New Mexico. The program we do is called the Theater of Enlightenment. As part of the program, we traditionally invite the larger community, beyond the group we are working with, to join us. We offer a lecture about the labyrinth on Friday afternoon and then everyone is invited, in the evening, to join us for a labyrinth walk. In this case, we were in a relatively small room with a labyrinth design pattern on the floor and many people. And because of the participation of the monastery, many of the people were dressed in their white robes—creating a charismatic, fascinating quality.

Well, into this evening's walk comes a big, tall, rather good-looking man in his early forties—and I thought, "Hmm, he hasn't had instruction with the labyrinth." So I gave him my short thirty-second talk about the labyrinth and how the ritual entails walking along the path of the labyrinth from the entrance to its center—and then sitting or standing in the center for as long as you want, and then following the same path out.

And he seemed to me sort of surly, with a kind of "What the hell is this thing?" attitude. He walked into the labyrinth without following the path and I thought to myself, "Well, that's fine, he didn't follow the path." And then all of a sudden, I start hearing sobs. I look around to see what is happening— it's the man who came in, and he's racked with sobs, he's fallen to his knees, lying down on the labyrinth, sobbing and sobbing and sobbing.

This is not what's expected, or so it might seem. But you're holding a space for the consciousness of the group, and you're making sure that people are dealing with it. I'm not going to say, "Excuse me—you're interrupting the labyrinth walk." Instead, you go with whatever is, trusting whatever is arising. And whatever mystery is going to live itself out.

I think that's part of the issue about the magic and the mystery of the group—it is that you have to be really secure in yourself, to let whatever's going to live out, live out. And I call it holding the space, but you're holding your inner space too.

The man remains lying on the labyrinth for some twenty minutes and finally gets up. There is a sense of relief. He starts walking toward the exit and then suddenly turns around and goes right smack dab into the center of the labyrinth, crumples to the floor, and starts sobbing again, louder than before.

And then a group of people near him made a judgment, and it's a judgment that came from the group and from within the container of the labyrinth. It was a decision to begin a ritual for healing called "laying of hands." And they worked with him physically and energetically as he cried for another forty-five minutes or so until he reached the end of his pain for that time. During that time, no one else in the community could go into the center. They may have reached the center, but it was jammed with people and this man sobbing. During this process, I didn't do anything to stop what was happening. I just let it be, let the community handle it, which is part of holding the whole space. I learned later that he came because of a dream, was given guidance in his dream to come to this monastery.

And so what does this have to do with the community, with our group in the room? Here we are, with this man definitely in a crisis. And then it began to reveal itself, its meaning for the monastery, for the larger community, and the larger healing that is needed. Its significance is for everybody—what part of ourselves is racked in pain? What part of ourselves needs to come apart? Or when in our life have we been in that place? See, everything can be used.

One way I understood it was through Scripture—the "welcoming of the stranger." Now, we could have said, "Excuse me, you're not part of this program." Or, "Excuse me, you're being too emotional." All of the silly things that could have happened if you don't understand that there's mystery being lived out here.

Everyone was able to get something from this experience. To do this, however, you need to keep the energy unblocked, to clear the path for people to be able to understand its meaning in their own lives.

The stranger could be archetypal. There's a making room, even when you have the view, "Hey, this was my labyrinth walk;

excuse me, what are you doing here?" But metaphorically, I think it's about allowing, making room, receiving. Dropping your own agenda and seeing that there's a bigger agenda being lived out.

COMMENTARY

At one key moment of the story, Artress pointed to the wisdom that emerged in the group during the labyrinth ritual experience—the decision to turn toward healing the man in the center of the circle. As she says, this is not something that can be directed from outside. Her role was to support what was unfolding and to trust that the labyrinth functioned as a container on behalf of wholeness and healing.

The stranger, or outsider, was the metaphoric lens through which she understood the unexpected entering the group. The disturbance created by the man who crumpled to the floor became a symbolic flash point allowing the members of the monastery to see their own mission to serve the larger community, including possibly their own internal needs for healing.

Artress is very clear about the nature of *welcoming all that is arising.* The emergence of collective wisdom is associated with respect for an underlying connectedness that reveals itself over time. You cannot intervene by simply saying this should not be happening. She demonstrated a willingness to be in the presence of the unknown and to trust that positive growth could be an outcome. In doing so, she furthered the group's capacity for resilience, for overcoming obstacles and improvising what was needed. No one and no group can be immune to unforeseen events, but we can learn to embrace the unexpected as opportunities for deepening our sense of larger purpose and enhancing our clarity.

Two complementary elements of Artress's story are particularly instructive in preparing for collective wisdom's emergence. First is the element of design. Design is an essential component for allowing groups to interact in ways that support meaning and purpose. Although some might think of design as how something looks, it is more often about how something works. The labyrinth is a design for healing and meditation, and is particularly a good tool for groups because of the symbolic nature of walking a path together. How you hurry forward or slow down as you individually walk the labyrinth affects everyone else. In an analogous way, the design of social processes and organizational structures also carries meaning regarding how people will interact with each other. Design helps determine how well we will recognize our interconnectedness, and it is an essential component of preparing groups for wisdom's emergence.

People need to participate in designs that are thoughtful and structures that support the task of the group, but they need something else as well. The stance of welcoming all that arises is a commitment to the spontaneity of group experience. This is the complementary element that must be present for groups to create a greater likelihood of collective wisdom emerging.

Although it may seem paradoxical, we can prepare for spontaneity. We do this simply by not imposing on the group our outlook about how something should happen or how something could have been done better. As Artress described it, saying to the person sobbing that he is being too emotional is not helping the group to discover what is possible. Instead, she asks how this spontaneous occurrence might contribute to a better understanding of the group's situation. We are in the realm of group improvisation, which is exactly how Artress understood her own role to serve what was spontaneously unfolding. It was only by reminding herself that she was guardian of the collective experience that she had the restraint to not intervene.

The stance of welcoming all that arises is an attitude and bearing that demonstrates positive regard for the unknown and unexpected. It is fundamental skill in any collective process because predictably the unexpected happens. Collective wisdom is far more likely to arise when individuals and groups can embrace events rather than recoil in fear or anger. This does not imply a posture of forced delight but a thoughtfulness and understanding that every outer event has an inner meaning and orientation. This is what Lauren Artress modeled so well through her inner preparation and understanding of symbol and metaphor. When we prepare ourselves to follow where the unexpected leads, we are better able to develop the resourcefulness necessary for life's challenges.

S E E I N G   W H O L E   S Y S T E M S / S E E K I N G
D I V E R S E   P E R S P E C T I V E S

The stance of *seeing whole systems/seeking diverse perspectives* shifts our attention from the individual to the group. In the earlier stories by Paula Underwood, Jacob Needleman, and Lauren Artress, we saw elements of this stance throughout their descriptions. Underwood demonstrated how to create empathic connections through deep listening. Needleman's portrait of the creation of the U.S. Constitution revealed how Franklin could see bickering factions but also a group birthing a historic design for democracy. Artress recognized how a leader can design an event and still embrace the unplanned element, seeing diversity in the form of a stranger who is still understood as part of the larger system.

Each group member sees the world in a unique way, but all the information is valuable and part of the whole. Sometimes this is uncomfortable because diverse views and fundamentally different approaches conflict and constrain a group's ability to adapt and change. Nonetheless, these diverse perspectives matter because they reveal more of the whole system. Committing to this stance requires patience and persistence. It also requires us to pay attention to how we pay attention. In other words, if we look for what separates us from each other and what problems groups have, we will certainly find it. If we look for what unites us and what is already working in a group, we can find that too. Learning to notice how and what we pay attention to matters. It is one of the keys for increasing the likelihood that collective wisdom will emerge.

A number of years ago, business author David Dorsey interviewed Jerry Sternin about his time in Vietnam, where he had done remarkable work involving childhood malnutrition in rural Vietnamese villages. The article that came from their collaboration, published in *Fast Company*, further defined Sternin's ideas about a systemic intervention called *positive deviance*. It is an illustration of how paying attention to a whole system and seeking out what is working can make a huge difference.

Positive Deviance

Based on a story of Jerry Sternin's work with
childhood malnutrition in Vietnam [13]

AT THE INVITATION OF THE Vietnamese government, Jerry Sternin went to Vietnam in the 1990s to work on eradicating malnutrition in the country's villages as a staff member of Save the Children. Building on research by Marian Zeitlin of Tufts University, he held the kernel of an idea and a question: Is it possible to find out why some children might be healthy? This was a very odd question when everyone knew their mission was to fight the problem of malnutrition against near-hopeless odds, with its attendant and well-documented poverty, poor sanitation, limited food distribution systems, lack of access to fresh water, and political bureaucracy. Who in their right mind would ask if anyone was well nourished?

Well, that is exactly what Sternin did. He stood in front of a group of women from a local village who had been trained to chart the growth of the children by age and weight. He asked them if there were any children under three who were from poor families but well nourished. He did not know what would happen next. The answer was like the call and response of birds singing to each other. "*Co* [pronounced "Gah," meaning "Yes"], *co, co*."

"You mean it's possible today in this village for a very poor family to have a well-nourished child?" Sternin asked them.

"*Co, co, co*" was the answer. And then all of them went off to see for themselves. "That's how it starts," said Sternin: The change began with the impulse to see what was happening before anything changed.

What they found was that the families that maintained healthy children adopted, in slight but meaningful ways, habits that were modifications of the norm. The norm in most villages was that families, when faced with limited food, would reduce their number of meals in direct proportion to the amount of available food. If there was plenty of food, they'd eat three or four times a day. When there was less food, twice a day; and with very limited food, just once a day. Under these circumstances, families were almost always malnourished.

Contrasting with this pattern, the healthy families ensured that children ate small portions many times a day. They went into the rice paddies to collect tiny shrimp that could be mixed in with the rice, and into the fields to collect sweet potato greens, a food that many looked down upon. They displayed directive and nurturing behaviors, such as making sure the children actually ate the food. And they went against the conventional wisdom by feeding even the children with diarrhea, small portions but consistently. Sternin began to grasp the importance of being specific, understanding exactly what made the outcome work. He was learning from the part of the system that was adapting and becoming successful.

"In every community, organization, or social group," wrote David Dorsey about the meaning of Sternin's findings, "there are individuals whose exceptional behaviors or practices enable them to get better results. . . . Without realizing it, these 'positive deviants' have discovered the path to success for the entire group—that is, if their secrets can be analyzed, isolated, and then shared with the rest of the group." For example, the conventional wisdom was to limit feedings, avoid certain foods for reasons of status, and eliminate feedings during bouts of diarrhea. Yet an alternative behavior, found within the group itself, held the possibility of survival.

Sternin wisely chose not to overemphasize the success of the few but rather to treat them as scouts of the collective. The solutions that were necessary could not be reduced to a formula and taught to others by experts. Instead, those who practiced successfully had to be the ones to teach the new behaviors. The guiding question for the methodology was how to enlarge the network. How do you amplify successful behaviors by making the group the "guru" of change?

The emphasis was on productive relationships and encouraging new behavior. As an illustration of this approach, a health volunteer would invite eight to ten mothers into her home to participate in and learn about medicinal food preparation. In order to come, the mothers would have to collect tiny shrimp and crab and the sweet potato greens. For two weeks they prepared food together and then continued the practices within their own homes. In cases where families did not have success, they were welcomed back for another two-week period. The bias was always toward action, calibration, and remaining true to the actual circumstances of the situation.

"We call conventional wisdom about malnutrition," Sternin reflected about his learning, "true but useless." He feels the same way about most organizational change strategies that rely on outside expertise alone. "The traditional model for social and organizational change doesn't work. It never has. You can't bring permanent solutions in from outside." Instead, Sternin works from inside the system, learning what are considered the acceptable behaviors of the majority while continually seeking the "positive deviants" who represent an alternative solution.

When Sternin and his wife went to Vietnam, they were novices, "like orphans at the airport when we arrived. . . . We had no idea what we were going to do." Without presumption of an answer, they were open to seeking new perspectives and disciplined about paying attention to what was already working. They knew they had to depend on the people closest to the situation and to respect that an appropriate response to malnutrition was already present in the village. From this orientation, they could listen with a kind of beginner's mind, curious and willing to ask lots of questions. "Our attitude was, Oh my God, what's going to happen?"

COMMENTARY

What happened was remarkable. There was a continual willingness to experiment, adjust, track results, and celebrate successes. The charting of children's growth by age and weight became common practice. The expectation that malnourishment could not be impacted was confronted, challenged, and altered by demonstrating success with quantitative studies. The work that began with 4 villages extended to 14 and ultimately to 265. In all, the work begun in Vietnam has touched over 2.2 million people and has been extended to over twenty countries.

Sternin's ideas demonstrate the value of directing attention to what is already working in groups, revealing a wisdom found through collective discovery and cooperative learning. The sound judgment cultivated in one part of the system can then be amplified through a larger network of individuals, through teams, and across communities of shared interest. Sternin discovered the immense power of the collective by inviting people to discover replicable aspects of solutions that mattered to them, rather than codifying protocols, enforcing norms from above, or trying to duplicate best practices from other villages.

The stance of seeing whole systems and seeking diverse perspectives is a commitment of inquiry and a willingness to suspend the conventional wisdom for new possibilities. The answers are available to us if we know how to turn our attention to those who already embody some part of the solution. Committing to this stance requires us to practice what the business writer Dorsey called Sternin's "beginner's mind."

At its most basic, it is the readiness to listen and ask lots of questions.

Collective wisdom is more likely to arise when we do not see ourselves as experts separated from others. We may bring expertise to a group, but groups develop the know-how they need when they make discoveries for themselves. The Vietnamese women, for example, whose growth and weight charts pointed to families with healthy children could not be held back from learning more. The information they discovered was then amplified by more experiments, more data collection, and recruiting of new followers. The role of individuals is to further the efforts of the group by constantly seeking to encourage new behavior—tapping into the extraordinary power for innovation and adaptation already present in groups and communities.

TAKING A STANCE ON BEHALF OF COLLECTIVE WISDOM

The meaning of life is not a fact to be discovered,
but a choice that you make about the way you live.

—Hilda Bernstein, South African activist

The power of collective wisdom is evidenced by what is accomplished. Are the decisions we make in accordance with deeper values? Have we made room for the opinions of others in order to find shared understanding? Do we inquire about the larger system by seeking diverse perspectives? How well do we welcome outsiders into our group? When dissent arises, can we listen well and seek common ground? What is done to find constructive possibilities when the conventional wisdom tells us not to bother? The short answer for how best to prepare for collective wisdom is to take a stance. Our choices, commitments, and convictions define the meaning of our lives and prepare us to be with others in ways that deny or amplify wisdom.

What aids collective wisdom's emergence is an awareness and respect for our underlying connectedness—to each other, nature, and spirit. As revealed through these stories from an Iroquois clan mother, a Western philosopher, a spiritual teacher, and a social activist, collective wisdom is a culmination of group behaviors. We prepare for collective wisdom by the quality of how we listen, by using our logical mind and our symbol-making intelligence, by valuing the future in the choices we make in the moment. We prepare for collective wisdom when we refrain from hardening our opposition to others and reframe our circumstances. The choices we make are embodied in the stances we take. It matters that we think deeply about the design of how people interact with each other: the physical structure, norms, and aspirations we create and hold together. It matters that there is space for spontaneity, caring behaviors, and ways to esteem others.

We are conduits for collective wisdom to arise when as individuals and groups we learn to pay attention to how we pay attention. What parts of a larger system do we see and not see? How skilled are we in methods of inquiry? Do we notice what is working? We have the ability to question and reflect on our own as well as collective behavior, and this has proved to be an extraordinary advantage.

A theme weaves through these stories of an indigenous people learning together over ten thousand years, a document for democracy that has lasted over two centuries, a design that remains vital after five thousand years. The theme is that human beings have knowledge of themselves as individuals and as members of a collective. We have the ability to reflect personally, to bend back the gaze of our own mind and observe our own thoughts, just as we can observe collectively the behavior of a group while still a member of it. We can, though never without struggle, transcend our habitual behaviors. We can innovate when necessary and alter our collective direction as a group, a nation, a human species. The stances we take define us and provide us with meaning.

If we step back from any one particular stance, we can also glimpse a larger pattern. The stances we create for ourselves—the internal perspectives we choose and the external actions we take—arise from our way of looking at the world. How we look at the world matters. How we observe and understand our own worldview matters.

If we see a world of pure chance and limited resources, of hostile enemies and heartless human actions, then the stances we discuss in this chapter, such as deep listening, seeking diverse perspectives, welcoming all that is arising, and trusting in the transcendent, become mottos without meaning. We are left to fend for ourselves. Our thoughts are directed from the outside by immediate threats and from the inside by fear, anger, and the desire to protect ourselves or to dominate others. It is a worldview unfortunately all too familiar.

The stances that support the emergence of collective wisdom arise from a far different framework of beliefs. It is a worldview of intimate connectivity, of shared power as our greatest adaptive advantage, and of a regard for individual genius not separate from collective accomplishment. It is this subject of worldview, with its relationship to collective wisdom, that we look at next.

three

Inhabiting a Different Worldview

In the early 1970s, one of our colleagues, Robert Kenny,
helped develop and lead educational and mental health
programs for youth in New York City. Inspired by the work
of the visionary educator Erling Thunberg, Kenny began to
put into practice the values of community, personal authenticity, and collaborative leadership advocated by Thunberg.
He noticed that even casual visitors to these youth programs commented on the "palpable atmosphere, or field,
that they sensed—the therapeutic milieu, as we used to call
it."[1] Many of the students' public school teachers expressed
amazement that these students, engaged and focused, were
the same kids they knew to be violent and destructive.

Kenny became fascinated with what Thunberg referred to as "group consciousness." He wondered if indeed his transformative experience in New York, which was healing and creative for so many, might be a portal to a different way of understanding life that involved work as a spiritual practice, collective consciousness, and group wisdom. Like Thunberg and so many other pioneers in social experimentation of that time, he was challenged to think differently about the meaning of the explosive changes going on in technology, communications, culture, and human values.

Collective wisdom, as a field of study and practice, is a different worldview than the more common mechanistic worldview, in which clear chains of causality can be constructed, analyzed, and dissected into their smallest parts. As Kenny suspected, we have begun to understand a far more complex and living world in which individuals have the power to join together with others and take stances that move us collectively toward cooperation, healing, and creative acts. Rather than being subject to external rules and ideological frameworks that dictate our reality, we are far more responsible for our world and worldview than we realized. Kenny's breakthrough thinking was that there are other ways of understanding human reality than the machine metaphor that so often rules our thought.

FIVE SOCIAL VISIONARIES WHO CONTRIBUTED TO THE FIELD OF COLLECTIVE WISDOM

Collective wisdom is constructed from a worldview that invites relationship and a deepening regard for our underlying connectedness. By worldview, we mean simply a framework of beliefs and perspectives that mold the way we see the world. A worldview on behalf of collective wisdom, however, is not a specific set of beliefs but a coherent value system that demands continuing study, dialogue, and reflection. It requires a knack for seeing patterns, breaking with established norms, and an ability to step back and see the whole.

Fortunately, many scholars, teachers, and practitioners have cultivated the soil before us. We have chosen a small group of them to aid our journey. Like most of us, they struggled with what they were finding; and at times they were misunderstood, ignored, and in some cases ridiculed and had their writings banned. Yet they persisted. They were individuals constructing a worldview that recognized the collective nature underlying human relationships and the deep alignment of natural systems and human organization. They were visionaries and early adopters of disciplines now described as the *new sciences* embodied in quantum physics, neurocognitive research, chaos theory, and the theory of self-organizing systems.

Each portrait of a social visionary that follows is associated with a critical aspect of collective wisdom. Carl Jung and Albert Einstein examine the acausal nature of reality, exploring phenomena such as meaningful coincidence and universal consciousness. The stance of welcoming all that is arising takes on added significance when even chance events may be portals to greater collective meaning. The priest and scientist Pierre Teilhard de Chardin embodies the stance we described as seeing whole systems/seeking diverse perspectives. He offers a hypothesis that there exists a field of thought, analogous to the biosphere, that surrounds and permeates our individual thought. Mary Parker Follett, a management consultant of the early twentieth century, puts forward an alternative to traditional hierarchies based on dominance and highlights the need for reciprocity in human relationships. Finally, Ralph Waldo Emerson gives expression to the codevelopment of individual consciousness and human association in groups, stressing the fundamental alignment of human thought, nature, and cosmos. Taken together, these men and women were exploring the roots of our collective humanity, the wisdom of our human species, and the challenges of our future evolution.

Crossing disciplines and penetrating deeply into the nature of reality, they explored fields as far ranging as physics, physical anthropology, philosophy, psychology, religion, and social organization. Their work was also a continuation of a historical conversation going back hundreds, even thousands of years. Their ideas joining collectivity and wisdom were influenced by spiritual and philosophical traditions dating back to cultural and indigenous traditions from around the globe. From the ancient compositions of the Upanishads of India to the insights of the Tao Te Ching in China, to the philosophical writings of Plato, to the enlightenment traditions found among Jews, Christians, Muslims, Hindus, Buddhists, and nonbelievers, they were building from a worldview that was inclusive of human and transworldly elements.

These thinkers were influenced by modern science as well, with the emphasis on discovering truth, allowing neither faith in past dogma nor reliance on past traditions to bar them from uncovering new ideas. As pioneers of collective wisdom, they offer us a prism through which to see ourselves and to build further. They aid us in understanding what is so compelling about seeking new perspectives and why it is so necessary to develop the binocular vision we need in order to see the world both collectively and with wisdom.

SYNCHRONICITY: A WORLDVIEW OF MEANINGFUL COINCIDENCE

Carl Gustav Jung (July 26, 1875–June 6, 1961) was a Swiss psychiatrist and the originator of concepts such as the collective unconscious, synchronicity, and psychological archetypes. He was an investigator of patterns and relationships common to dreams, art, mythology, philosophy, and religion.

Albert Einstein (March 14, 1879–April 18, 1955) was a German-born theoretical physicist best known for his theory of relativity.

IT COULD EASILY BE A scenario from a mystery thriller. It is early in the twentieth century and the setting is a metropolitan European city. Carl Jung, a young, accomplished physician, lectures on the unconscious. It is a new and different idea beginning to attract serious consideration in intellectual circles. Jung stays up into the night talking with friends, although he is, for no apparent reason, feeling unusually restless and nervous. Something is bothering him, but he continues to socialize with his colleagues.

Around midnight, he returns to his room but is unable to fall asleep. Minutes and hours tick off the clock until finally he begins to doze off, only to be awakened with a start. He senses that someone is in the room with him and quickly turns on the lamp by his bed. He is almost certain that the door to his room was opened, and he gets up, opens the door, and peers out into the corridor. There is no one, only a deathly stillness. Attempting to re-create the sequence of events that startled him awake, he recalls being awakened by a dull pain as if struck in the forehead and then again in the back of his skull. What is going on?

Jung returns to bed and sleeps fitfully. The following day, he learns that one of his patients has committed suicide, firing a bullet into his own skull. The scenario of a mystery thriller deepens and turns into reality. Jung, believing that his experience the night before was some form of psychic phenomenon, begins to imagine the possibility that the event revealed an instance of distance telepathy, a warp in the fabric of time and space.

Carl Jung, the young physician of the psyche, sensed a connection between his own ideas involving causality and those of an even younger man, the physicist Albert Einstein.

Between 1909 and 1913, the two men, still in their thirties, met for dinner at Jung's home in Zurich. It was in these early conversations that Jung began to glimpse an analogy between the atom and the psyche. Both contained enormous quantities of energy, and both were being revealed as having hidden qualities. And most significantly, both were subject to larger, invisible *fields*. Listening to Einstein address his fascination with relativity theory, Jung began to form what would become his own theory of synchronicity—an acausal connecting principle. Synchronicity, an idea that Jung developed with the quantum physicist and Nobel laureate Wolfgang Pauli, posed the possibility that meaningful coincidences might have psychic explanations and not solely causal ones. Time and space were relative. Synchronicity, like quantum theory in physics, challenged the very foundations of classical science. It represented an unbroken wholeness in which even apparently unrelated events were woven together in a continuous fabric.

Synchronicity invites us to pay attention to the entirety of experience and to be fully present, because every moment and chance event may have meaning. While a traditional approach to decision making may be to analyze pros and cons, classifying, selecting, and isolating variables, the mind less tethered sees a fuller, more connected whole. We give ourselves permission to consider how outer events may have inner meaning. We recognize the added value in reflection on metaphor and symbol, and this gives birth to fresh perspectives. New insights emerge through the act of seeking patterns and relationships among variables that would be "off the grid" for a more traditional and constrained observer.

This idea that individual awareness is part of a continuous stream of collective consciousness is easy enough to consider but disorienting to grasp. Jung wrote about ideas like synchronicity to highlight the ways in which our notions of reality are often limiting, too easily bounded by fixed ideas and categories of separation. He had come to see that classical physics was built on a house of cards—that the certainty of such concepts as atoms moving in predictable billiard-ball-like fashion was false. Quantum physics operated on shifting sands much more like his own ideas of the unconscious, an *uncertainty principle* that made probabilities more relevant than precise predictability. And like David Bohm, the quantum physicist who described reality as emerging from an *implicate order*, Jung believed there was a larger unbroken wholeness from which psychic patterns manifested.

Collective wisdom as a worldview is similarly a break with classical ideas of group behavior that are defined by singular determinants such as motivation, leadership, or interpersonal communication. It is instead an expression of the belief that there exists a field of collective consciousness—often seen and expressed through metaphor—that is real and influential, yet invisible. Collective wisdom is an orientation embedded in nature, the nature of the physical world and our own human nature. It is therefore dependent on a keen sensitivity to the natural world and our powers of observation, mediated through our senses: touch, sight, sound, smell, and taste. Yet it is also a commitment to an open-ended inquiry and understanding found beyond the established modes of conventional perception, beyond ordinary sensory experience.

Premonitions and Extraordinary Ways of Knowing

There is a wonderful story reported by Laurens van der Post, an Afrikaner and colleague of Jung's. He was one of the first whites of that nation to decry the tragic consequences of in-equality between whites and blacks in South Africa that led to apartheid. And he also decried the inequality within our own psyche that elevated human traits of rationality and ab-straction over the instinctual and collective. As a child, he was fascinated by stories of the Kalahari Bushmen, a vanish-ing group of extraordinary hunters who descended from the most ancient of our human ancestry.

IN 1955, THE BBC COMMISSIONED van der Post to make a docu-mentary of the Bushmen, which led to his most well-known nonfiction work, *The Lost World of the Kalahari*. In it, he de-scribes his time with Dabe, a Bushman, and their hunting of a giant eland, the largest of the world's antelopes. Returning to camp, van der Post asked Dabe what his people would say when they saw the success of the hunt. Dabe, who had had contact with the outside world, told him with assurance, "They already know." "What on earth do you mean?" asked van der Post.

Dabe told him they knew by "wire," using the English word for the telegraph he had once seen when accompa-nying a white man into the city. "We Bushman have a wire here," he said, tapping his chest, "that brings us news." Much later, as they approached the camps, van der Post could hear the women singing. "Do you hear?" Dabe asked van der Post. "They're singing 'The Eland Song.'"[2]

The Kalahari is thousands of miles from Princeton, the elite American university in New Jersey, but there at the Institute of Advanced Study, Jung's dinner guest from an earlier period was contemplating very similar matters. At approximately the same time (between 1954 and 1955) when Dabe was tapping his chest, Albert Einstein was putting into words his intuition about the cosmos and our place in it. He wrote,

> A human being is a part of the whole, called by us "Universe," a part limited in time and space. He experiences himself, his thoughts and feelings as something separated from the rest, a kind of optical delusion of his consciousness. This delusion is a kind of prison for us, restricting us to our personal desires and to affection for a few persons nearest to us. Our task must be to free ourselves from this prison by widening our circle of compassion to embrace all living creatures and the whole of nature in its beauty. Nobody is able to achieve this completely, but the striving for such achievement is in itself a part of the liberation and a foundation for inner security.[3]

Einstein, who never fully accepted an acausal explanation for reality, nevertheless saw our deep interconnection. Separateness is the optical delusion of our divided consciousness. Our thoughts and feelings appear to be a private affair, but they are intimately bound up with others. He asked himself how such cosmic religious feelings could be communicated among human beings even if those feelings could not give rise to a definitive notion of God or any particular theology. His answer was that this was the role of art and science—to awaken in us a deep regard for our connectedness to each other and a larger universe. This is a form of aesthetic sensibility, an eminently moral and practical worldview that nourishes our natural curiosity and humanity. It is a conviction and act of mindfulness captured brilliantly in modern times by our colleague Parker Palmer:

> We are participants in a vast communion of being, and if we open ourselves to its guidance, we can learn anew how to live in this great and gracious community of truth. We can and we must—if we want our sciences to be humane, our institutions to be sustaining, our healings to be deep, our lives to be true.[4]

Jung's Final Days

During the final days of Carl Jung's life, he received a visit by the Chilean writer Miguel Serrano, a colleague. They talked about the fact that ideas could persist under different names but what was essential was the worldview, the framework of realities that lay underneath the labels. "What I have done in my work," Jung told Serrano, "is simply to give new names to those ideas, to those realities. Consider, for example, the word 'Unconscious.' I have just finished reading a book by a Chinese Zen Buddhist. And it seemed to me that we were talking about the same thing, and that the only difference between us was that we gave different words to the same reality. Thus the use of the word Unconscious doesn't matter; what counts is the idea that lies behind the word."[5]

Jung was giving voice to an awareness that ideas lie out-side the individual mind but can be discovered and rediscov-ered (by individuals) from different disciplines and different cultural backgrounds. To inhabit a worldview of such shared collective knowing, we need to be able to hold in our mind a larger canvas on which to see the cumulative accomplish-ments of consciousness. We need to understand ourselves as a human species evolving together. Possibly, this thought was inspired by another book that Jung was reading. Asked by Serrano about a book on his bedside table, Jung, pale yet seemingly illuminated by an inner light, turned to Teilhard de Chardin's work *The Human Phenomenon* and commented, "It is a great book."

A WORLDVIEW OF INTIMATE CONNECTIVITY

Pierre Teilhard de Chardin, S.J. (May 1, 1881–April 10, 1955) was a French Jesuit priest trained as a paleontologist and a phi-losopher. His writings sought to reconcile science and the sacred. He is best known for his book *Le Phénomène humain* (translated as both *The Human Phenomenon* and *The Phenom-enon of Man*) and for his concept of an enveloping conscious-ness he described as the *noosphere*.

Collective wisdom draws from the breadth and depth of human knowledge, permeated with the presence of spirit. No doubt a fault line has divided these worlds—a split be-tween religious faith and scientific understanding, between a call for material progress and a reawakening of spiritual in-sight. Even in an area as basic as our description of physical matter, views differ as to whether it is inanimate or suffused with consciousness. Yet we each can have a say in reconciling these worlds, creating a larger worldview that can embrace both.

One pioneer of this exploration was the twentieth-century French priest Pierre Teilhard de Chardin. Seeking to communicate his unique way of perceiving the world, Teilhard wrote, "It has been my destiny to stand at a privileged crossroads in the world; there, in my twofold character of priest and scientist, I have felt passing through me, in particularly exhilarating and varied conditions, the double stream of human and divine forces."[6]

"Varied conditions" indeed! Teilhard was born amid the volcanic landscape of Auvergne in the ancient central province of France. He taught physics in Cairo; studied theology in Sussex, England; worked in a paleontology laboratory in Paris; and was part of the excavation of prehistoric painted caves in northwest Spain. At midlife, he spent much of two decades in China and Mongolia, participating in the discovery of Peking Man; and he died finally in New York City. All the while, he wrote to loved ones, kept numerous journals, and sought to realize his vision in books that were suppressed by the Catholic Church in Rome. Teilhard's thoughts began to circulate more forcefully after his death in 1955, when his first book was published in the United States as *The Phenomenon of Man* (1959).

Teilhard wanted to tell us of a vision most famously quoted by Sargent Shriver in his acceptance speech as the U.S. Democratic vice presidential candidate in 1972. Shriver, the first director of the Peace Corps, ended his speech with these words from Teilhard's *Toward the Future*: "The day will come when, after harnessing space, the winds, the tides, gravitation, we shall harness for God the energies of love. And, on that day, for the second time in the history of the world, man will have discovered fire."[7]

From the Trenches of War, a New Spirit Rising

IT SEEMS AN ODD PLACE for an epiphany, but many of Teilhard's key ideas began to arise in him during his time in the trenches as a stretcher bearer in World War I. Carting the dead and wounded from the front lines, in the midst of war's chaos, he began to sense new meaning from a mass of humanity crowding in on itself. He began to perceive humankind as a single whole, a cosmic reality that transcended individuals or nations. "I have just been watching the moon rise over the crest of the nearby trenches," he wrote in 1918. "The timid slim crescent of earlier evenings has gradually grown to a full and shining disc. Solitary and majestic, the moon, which a fortnight before had been invisible, disengaged itself from the ridges of black soil, and seemed to glide across the barbed wire. In this shining body that hangs in the heavens I greet a new symbol. . . . Is it the moon that rises over the dark trenches this evening, or is it the earth, a unified earth, a new earth?"[8]

Teilhard began to distinguish a phylum, to borrow a phrase from biology, or grouping that joined together all humankind despite the particular qualities of any individual or group. And what made this grouping distinctive was the capacity for reflection, an inward quality that continues to evolve even as the physical body remains constant. He named this quality the *within* of human life, made possible by the unique arrangement of the human nervous system and infused with psychic life. Humans were at once utterly unique and undoubtedly part of a collective. Teilhard saw these two forces coming together consciously, catalyzed by the power of reflection, the within of spirit radiating outward.

> In the eyes of the physicist, nothing exists legitimately, at least up to now, except the without of things. The same intellectual attitude is still permissible in the bacteriologist, whose cultures . . . are treated as laboratory reagents. But it is still more difficult in the realm of plants. It tends to become a gamble in the case of a biologist studying the behaviour of insects or coelenterates. It seems merely futile with regard to the vertebrates. Finally, it breaks down completely with man, in whom existence of a within can no longer be evaded, because it is the object of a direct intuition and the substance of all knowledge.[9]

Human reality was inherently collective, a living dynamic organism, and an immense network of associations threading itself across the globe. The evolution of the collective human advanced in fits and starts but was informed by an exquisite reciprocity between individual psychic life and the human phylum as a whole. The human organism evolved in the direction of cooperation, driven by advancing knowledge of the cosmos on the one hand and by ever-intensifying psychosocial interaction on the other. The word that Teilhard eventually used to describe this vision of intimate connectivity was *noosphere*, analogous to *biosphere*, a term coined by the geologist Eduard Suess.

The biosphere was the ecological pattern of air, surface rock, water, and land that formed an envelope where life dwelled. For Teilhard, the noosphere was a similar ecological pattern in which human thought resided. He saw a human collective, coiled together, living within this larger envelope of thought and informed by the within of spirit. The growth of collective knowledge, imperceptible to the eye, was being accelerated by particular problems of life needing solutions on a global scale. Beyond the immediate crises of his time, Teilhard foresaw the global challenges of sustaining the earth's life-giving resiliency, the requirements of an increasing world population, and the demands of a human species driven by both material and spiritual hunger. Collective awareness was advanced by an interactive accumulation, meaning accelerating human interaction on the one hand and recognition of the urgency to address the needs of the planet on the other. The noosphere, ignited by human reflection, was a vision of global connectivity and integration. The result was an increased intensity and sophistication of human thought. He wrote,

> A glow ripples outward from the first spark of conscious reflection. The point of ignition grows larger. The fire spreads in ever widening circles till finally the whole planet is covered with incandescence. Only one interpretation, only one name can be found worthy of this grand

phenomenon. Much more coherent and just as extensive as any preceding layer, it is really a new layer, the "thinking layer," which, since its germination at the end of the Tertiary period, has spread over and above the world of plants and animals. In other words, outside and above the biosphere there is the noosphere.[10]

The capacity of inner reflection, advanced by an evolving nervous system, lifted the human species from its humble beginnings as a single-celled organism. From this spark of consciousness, the human phenomenon began its journey. Social maturation, coming much later in the evolutionary chain, was the next major leap: "As far back as we can meet them," Teilhard wrote, "our great-great ancestors are to be found in groups and gathered round the fire."[11] In conversation, through social discourse, we begin to realize what it means to be a human species with the implicit challenges and opportunities that arise from such awareness. There is a dawning awareness that we can operate together. We can *cooperate*. But for what aims?

On another part of the planet, during roughly the same period of time that Teilhard was glimpsing a new earth rising above the trenches of warfare, a woman named Mary Parker Follett was formulating her thoughts on power and participatory democracy. She wrote pointedly about the need for a "co-active" power that Robert Kenny, more than a half-century later, would have found utterly familiar with his experience of collaborative leadership in New York City. Kenny,

Teilhard, and Follett shared a worldview different from one in which power is viewed as key to dominance over others. They saw how power might be constructively shared and directed toward positive aims.

A WORLDVIEW OF COCREATIVE POWER

Mary Parker Follett (1868–1933) was an American social worker, business consultant, and author of books on democracy, creative experience, and management. She wrote about the power of the collective that arises from shared power—*power with* as distinct from *power over*.

Follett grasped that a major impediment to thinking collectively about power is the fear of subordination to others. Radically, she believed that this fear comes from the all-too-common experience of power being in the service of dominance. In contrast, she argued that only when we join ourselves vitally with others in arrangements of shared power can we reach a new threshold of cocreativity and purpose. Like Teilhard, she understood that this kind of power can come only from individuals' finding what is unique about themselves in order to best contribute to a healthier whole. She advanced the idea that it is our differences and our diversity that make the collective engine powerful. "Democracy," she wrote, "in fact insists on what are usually thought of as inequalities. Of course I am not 'as good as you'—it would be a pretty poor world if I were, that is if you were no better than I am. Democracy without humility is inconceivable."[12] Who was this systems thinker with a sharp tongue and a paradoxical bent?

A Prophet of Management and Collective Wisdom Ignored

In 1951, Peter Drucker, appointed a year earlier as a professor of management at New York University, was working on a manuscript that included his thoughts on dissent and conflict. Showing it to the English management pioneer Lyndall Urwick, he was surprised to hear Urwick suggest that it sounded a lot like the work of Mary Parker Follett.

"Mary who?" Drucker responded.[13]

During the early twentieth century, when consultants and businessmen such as Frederick Taylor, Henry Gantt, Frank Gilbreth, and Chester Barnard were championing standardization, time studies, and executive functions, Mary Parker Follett was whistling an entirely different tune. Long before it was fashionable, she was challenging the emphasis on external structures and engineering metaphors with ideas about living systems, aesthetic appreciation for design, and the inner vitality to be found within individuals and groups. She asked: How do you move from coercion and confrontational policies to respect for diversity and the power of collectivity? How do you move from the mindset of an engineer who controls all the variables to a vision of an ecosystem in which business is but one, albeit critical, social institution?

Born in Quincy, Massachusetts, three years after the Civil War ended, she graduated summa cum laude from Radcliffe College in 1898, having studied economics, government, law, and philosophy. Finishing her postgraduate education in Paris, she returned to work in Roxbury, Massachusetts, a section of Boston, where she turned ideas into practice as a social worker and community organizer. She was the first to conceive and implement the idea that the public school could act as a social hub, keeping the buildings open after hours for recreation and study. Seeing the connection between schooling and work, she helped create a model placement bureau for employment that was replicated throughout the Boston public school district.

For twenty-five years, she was associated with the development of community centers, adult learning, and social work. Her work was testament to what could be accomplished communally when the power of human association was welcomed and all sectors of society included. Building on these experiences, she authored articles and books, including *The New State: Group Organization the Solution of Popular Government* (1918) and *Creative Experience* (1924). In the 1920s and early 1930s, she was a sought-after speaker, giving lectures at the U.S. Bureau of Personnel Administration and at the London School of Economics' Department of Business Administration. Follett's writings were embraced in both Great Britain and Japan, foreshadowing participatory management, quality circles, and team-based approaches to group empowerment. Her writings heralded the current interest in learning organizations and anticipated the importance of both general systems theory and theories of emergence for group development and innovation. After learning of her work, Peter Drucker, who had asked who she was, rightly named her the "prophet" of management.

Follett was a prophet ignored. Yet her insights were recognized, then and now, as revolutionary. Lyndall Urwick recalled at the end of his life their first meeting: "In two minutes flat, I was at her feet and remained there till the day she died." Warren Bennis called her a "swashbuckling advance scout of management thinking." Rosabeth Moss Kanter of the Harvard Business School noted that reading Follett was "like entering a zone of calm in a sea of chaos. Her work reminds us . . . there are truths about human behavior that stand the test of time. They persist despite superficial changes, like the deep and still ocean beneath the waves of management fad and fashion."[14] Her ideas were ignored precisely because of their substance; they were subversive.

By the late 1930s and 1940s, with the confrontation of nations, fear of war, and heightened dependence on leaders in times of uncertainty, her advocacy of the group and collectives made her ideas seem foreign and uncomfortable to entertain. The climate of war and the rapid industrial growth that followed harbored little patience for understanding reciprocal relationship or mutual influence or how conflict might be an avenue for a higher order of resolution. Follett's sense of the aesthetic as a way of seeing patterns of wholeness, coherence, and beauty was at odds with the fragmentation of work and the desire for control. She was an advocate for collective wisdom before it had a name or a perceived need.

Pioneer, advance scout, and prophet of management, Follett understood that wisdom flows from principled ways of engaging collectivity, inclusive of all parts of society and deepened by the spirit of invitation. Her most lasting insights were about the nature of power and how traditional forms of power lead to dominance and submission but never to shared intention or innovation.

Power Over vs. Power With

Probably no idea is more essential to Follett's thinking than her distinction between *power over* and *power with*. *Power over* is a traditional relationship in which one person has power over another person or one group over another group or one nation over another nation. It is a traditional relationship in the sense that dominance and coercion are used time and again before other alternatives are sought. One side vies for power over another, at best trying to influence the other to concede its position, at worst using brute force to have its way. *Power over* is a relationship of polarity, opposite views and differentials in power forever attracting each other from a posture of suspicion if not downright contempt.

Power with is at once relational and collective. It creates new possibilities from the very differences that might exist in a group. Unlike brute force, which must be continually reinforced to sustain itself, *power with* emerges organically from the participants involved and grows stronger the more it is put to use. *Power with* is an organizational form of collaboration, an idea central to what today is called *stakeholder engagement, multisector approaches,* and *cocreative power*. *Power with* has the boldness to believe that acting from immediate self-interest is not always the wisest course of action, nor that one person or one group should be in a position to know what is best for another. Follett believed instead that reciprocal influence could lead to a creative synthesis. What is remarkable about Follett's approach is that she did not advance *power with* as a utopian solution. Rather, she asked a far simpler and subtler question: How could our dependence on relationships of *power over* be diminished?

Her inquiry led to three associated insights. First was seeing the possibility of integration, a way in which key desires from both sides of a polarity could be discerned and addressed. For this to happen, power had to be shifted and structures of one-sided influence had to give way to circular ones based on relationship. As each person, group, or nation sought to influence the other, it in turn was subject to influence. In this new way of approaching dialogue, legitimate concerns were revealed and new possibilities arose, becoming common ground for further action. "Throughout history," she wrote, "we see that control brings disastrous consequences whenever it outruns integration." Integration was achieved through relationship, candor, and an ability to see one's actions as part of a greater whole. She held that new organizational structures must be created to reinforce circular relationships of influence and was an early advocate for labor/management partnerships, still viewed as innovative today. Her point, however, was not that two sides find new ways to fight over their prerogatives but rather that they find shared ground and learn together from the transparency of data about their system.

This led to her second insight, which involved what she called the "law of the situation." Instead of marshaling outside experts and facts to bolster one side over the other, Follett proposed using information to advance transparency of operations. She saw the power of the scientific method, still nascent in her day, as useful in creating a shared pool of data that everyone could access. Trust could be gained by remaining true to actual operations, depending on those nearest to the situation, and mitigating errors before they could

mushroom. She held a bias toward action, recording the consequences, and calibrating new behaviors based on learning.
Follett saw this in the service of bringing forth a collective
will that could generate innovation and overcome obstacles
by honing a shared purpose.

Finally was her insight about leadership itself. She understood that true leaders do not command obedience through
force or manipulation but rather by giving expression to external realities and the interior aspirations of others. She
wrote,

> The skillful leader . . . does not rely on personal force; he
> controls his group not by dominating but by expressing
> it. He stimulates what is best in us; he unifies and con-
> centrates what we feel only gropingly and scatteringly,
> but he never gets away from the current of which we
> and he are both an integral part. He is a leader who gives
> form to the inchoate energy in every man. The person
> who influences me most is not he who does great deeds
> but he who makes me feel I can do great deeds. . . .
> Who ever has struck fire out of me, aroused me to action
> which I should not otherwise have taken, he has been
> my leader.[5]

Mary Parker Follett embodied the commitments and
convictions that give rise to collective wisdom. She foresaw
how critical was seeing the whole system, seeking diverse
perspectives and the role of respect in group discernment.
She believed deeply in what we have called the stances of
deep listening, suspension of certainty, welcoming all that

is arising, and trust in a transcendent mission. Most pointedly, she understood how and why reciprocal relations matter. Her work permeates our best thinking about power to
this day.

The Power of Direct Experience

IN 1927, FOLLETT WAS CONDUCTING a seminar at Harvard, grieving the loss of her beloved friend, Isobel Briggs. Feisty as ever,
though, she challenged her graduate students to learn by
watching and interpreting their own experience. "Experiment,
record, pool" was her motto, and she taught that from this
activity something new and vital could emerge. Her prior
lectures had summarized her advocacy of key principles for
coactive power, but now she wanted students to learn the
methodology that had led to her discoveries.

The students would have none of it. They saw only the
limitations of such effort. One asked what value this could be
without a prior conceptual framework. Another complained
that it was not possible to consider all the factors of a given
situation. A third questioned the utility of such action if Follett
had not given them explicit guidance on how to apply what
they were being taught. She responded pragmatically that
one should do as best as one could and that they were simply practicing paying attention to their own experience and
observations.

Finally, with some exasperation concerning their timidity
and cautiousness, she hit the roof:

> I think what I rather object to is this, that I have not sat
> and read books on philosophy and decided that the deep-

est fundamental principles of the universe were three. I have simply for about 25 years been watching boards and groups and have decided from that watching on these principles on interacting, unifying, and emerging. And it seems to me that you are supposing that I begin the other way around. In my experience that is what happens when you have fruitful results. I am giving my experience. I am not giving philosophy out of a book.[16]

Follett was giving voice to a methodology of how our worldview can be shaped by disciplined reflection on what we see, sense, feel, and observe. She was an early advocate of personal empowerment. Through this methodology of paying attention to one's own experience, we can begin to formulate discoveries together and see new patterns. The contribution each individual makes to the collective emerges from this commitment—to pay attention to inner experience and outer engagement with the world. "We are often told to 'surrender our individuality,'" she observed. "To claim our individuality is the one essential claim we have on the universe."[17]

It is not hard to imagine at least one former Harvard alumnus smiling down on the proceedings. Ralph Waldo Emerson had championed self-reliance as fundamental to the greater vision of the collective. For Emerson, like Follett, genius began with laying claim to one's talents in the service of a greater transcendent vision. It is his story we take up next.

A WORLDVIEW OF INDIVIDUAL CONTRIBUTION AND SHARED HUMANITY

Ralph Waldo Emerson (May 25, 1803–April 27, 1882) was an American philosopher, lecturer, essayist, poet, and leader of the Transcendentalist movement in the early and mid-nineteenth century.

Emerson's worldview embodied many of the convictions foundational to creating the likelihood of collective wisdom's emergence, and none more radiantly than the stance of trusting in the transcendent. He held a deep faith in the transcendent quality of human agency, in the awe and wonder of nature, and in transformation of human consciousness. The powers available to the individual, he believed, rested in the universal nature common to each of us.

Emerson's faith was tested early and often by life's unexpected and often tragic circumstances. His brother, John, died when Emerson was four, and his father died four years later. Ordained a Unitarian minister in 1829 after attending Harvard Divinity School, he accepted a ministerial role in Boston and married his eighteen-year-old sweetheart, Ellen Tucker. She was to be a poet in counterpoint to his being a preacher. Emerson was deeply in love, and the promising chords of life together were just beginning.

On February 8, 1831, just seventeen months after their marriage, Ellen died of tuberculosis. Over a year later, the twenty-eight-year-old Emerson visited her tomb, still grieving. He stood over her coffin and, in a practice unusual but not unheard of for that time, opened it. He had to see her and be near her. One of his biographers wrote that it was not a macabre action but one quintessential to Emerson. "Some part of him was not able to believe she was dead. He was still writing to her in his journals as though she was alive. . . . We do not know exactly what moved Emerson on this occasion, but we do know that he had a powerful craving for direct, personal, and unmediated experience."[18]

On Christmas Day of that same year, he sailed to Europe, eventually traveling to France. The voyage across the sea nearly killed him, and he recited to himself verses and phrases from *Lycidas* in which the poet Milton seemed to purge his doubts and fears in the very act of creating verse. Walking in the gardens of Paris, Emerson began to find his own melodic stride, experiencing an astonishment born from seeing an immeasurable diversity in nature, and beyond that a unity in a living cosmos.

Reverence in the Garden and Beyond

The Jardin des Plantes in Paris was far more than a botanical haven; it was a research center and natural history museum as well as Europe's gathering place for the study of plant classification. Walking through the flora and fauna gathered together, Emerson took in everything, from the botanical gardens, to exhibits of birds from all over the world, to displays of varied minerals: "grand blocks of quartz, native gold in all its forms and crystallization, threads, plate, crystals, dust and silver black as from fire."[19] Emerson's journals indicate the awe and inspiration he experienced:

Ah, said I, this is philanthropy, wisdom, taste,—to form a cabinet of natural history. The Universe is a more amazing puzzle than ever as you glance along this bewildering series of animated forms, the hazy butterflies, the carved shells, the birds, beasts, fishes, insects, snakes, and the upheaving principle of life everywhere incipient in the very rock aping organized forms.[20]

Everywhere he looked was more evidence of the web of life—the palpable connections between various specimens—and the rigor of research implicit in revealing this underlying unity. Here was the embryonic seed of his own vocational calling. He was to be a naturalist of the human phenomenon with one foot grounded in the earth and the other planted in a universal spirit. Emerson felt himself not simply an observer of nature but a participant and chronicler of his own interior nature. He experienced this as an embodied presence, powerfully expressed in his journal: "I feel the centipede in me—cayman, carp, eagle, and fox. I am moved by strange sympathies. I say continually, I will be a naturalist."[21] Nature, in all its beauty, savagery, and multiplicity, was not separate from the human experience, but a mirror expression of what lay within the human soul. And each soul was a conduit for something larger, something universal. How might he articulate this insight? How might he make this possible for others to see? Would anyone respond?

The Transcendentalist Club

RETURNING TO THE UNITED STATES, Emerson was on fire. He began a new career lecturing, remarried, and joined with a small group of people who were similarly disinclined to the aridness of Harvard's intellectual climate. They formed a club, later known as the Transcendentalist Club, whose one rule of membership was that no one's presence should restrain a topic from being discussed. The group, which encompassed ministers, philosophers, and educators as well as farmers, merchants, and mechanics, included Henry David Thoreau, Theodore Parker, Margaret Fuller, Amos and Abigail Alcott, Elizabeth Hoar, Sarah Ripley, and James Freeman Clarke, who later said, "We are called like-minded because no two of us think alike." The group fostered a great collaboration that allowed, in fact required, the distinctiveness of each person's unique gifts. Like a ring of giant sequoia trees, they provided each other the root system for the growth of the individual person.

Their conversations were permeated with the belief that humans are not the creators of those things we treasure most—justice, truth, love, and freedom. Rather, we are the receptive vessels in which the universal will expresses itself. Differing with each other on any specific topic, Emerson and his colleagues collectively expressed a desire for greater life, energy, and originality in human thought and activities. They sought to bridge diverse and often-competing perspectives, uniting spirituality with social reform, science with human intuition, and the study of nature with the magnificence of human thought. Their individual efforts and social awareness found resonance in the fields of education, theology, art, business, and what would later become collective efforts on behalf of the environment and social justice. Thoreau's small book on civil disobedience, for example, helped inspire Mohandas Gandhi's ideas on nonviolent resistance, which in turn inspired the works of Martin Luther King Jr. and Nelson Mandela.

Emerson's trust in human agency was infused with a transcendent element. The individual who awakens to a universal soul within empowers his or her imagination, radiating a magnetic message out into the world. Reverence for nature and spirit permeate Emerson's poetic language. Look upon a river and be reminded of the constant flux of reality; throw a stone in a stream and witness how influence is reproduced in a circle of repetitions. In each of us lies a universal mind. When we affirm this universal spirit, our message is amplified a hundredfold and cuts across time. We become conduits and conductors of universal meaning.

A Social Vision of Personal Contribution

Too often, we are asked to surrender precisely that which makes us distinctive. Emerson was clear that it was a trade-off that aided neither individual nor group, and how we resolved this paradox required a codevelopment of each. Championing self-reliance, Emerson was simultaneously one of the strongest advocates for the power of human association.

Emerson embraced the full spectrum of life, its contradictions and anomalies, as a necessary path for learning. He
famously perceived a crack in everything God had made,
which left us unfinished but also let light in. He advocated
that the light of spirit be joined with involvement in the
world, guided by a trust in one's own talents—one's own
true instincts. Such a stance draws people together and awakens the spirit in others. Such a stance has immeasurable energy and attractive powers. In groups, such as his experiment
with the Transcendentalist Club, we become not more like
the others, but more like ourselves.

"Every spirit builds itself a house," wrote Emerson in the
crescendo that ends *Nature*, the book that sprouted from his
walk in the Jardin des Plantes,

> and beyond its house a world; and beyond its world, a
> heaven. Know then, that the world exists for you. For
> you is the phenomenon perfect. What we are, that only
> can we see. All that Adam had, all that Caesar could,
> you have and can do. Adam called his house, heaven
> and earth; Caesar called his house, Rome; you perhaps
> call yours, a cobbler's trade; a hundred acres of ploughed
> land; or a scholar's garret. Yet line for line and point for
> point, your dominion is as great as theirs, though with-
> out fine names. Build, therefore, your own world.[22]

This was the Emersonian stone that rippled outward
into the stream of collective consciousness. Each of us is a
creator of worlds, each of us individually and collectively has

the power to reflect back a vision of truth, justice, beauty, love, and freedom. We should not fear what others think of us. Skip your stone across the generations of time. Each of us is blessed.

But are we? Some readers may rightly wonder why, if there is so much wisdom available to us, we have so much evidence of its opposite. How is it that groups and larger collectives can feel more like traps than portals to a new consciousness? We take up these questions more fully in our next chapters.

four

What Makes Groups Foolish

G roups that realize their potential for collective wisdom can experience moments of profound connection and become capable of extraordinary action. It barely
needs to be said, however, that this is not always the case.
Often, when human beings gather in groups, we become
conduits for wisdom's opposite—folly. We use the term
folly to reflect a continuum of behaviors from mere foolishness to acts of evil. Put bluntly, if human beings have the
capacity to access collective wisdom, why don't we? Why
are we so often responsible for collective foolishness or
worse? Why do we become enmeshed, again and again, in
seemingly endless cycles of petty and profound violence?

One answer to these questions is straightforward: Like wisdom, folly is an innate potential of human beings. Like collective wisdom, therefore, collective folly is a potential of all groups, not simply those groups we might label as dysfunctional or unhealthy, or groups that hold overtly destructive aims. Collective folly is a lived reality, and a legacy of thousands of years of conflict and warfare. Every day, human beings commit small acts of foolishness, conscious and unconscious acts of injustice, and unspeakable acts of violence and cruelty, within our families and among friends, against our peers and subordinates, and against groups of strangers small and large that we deem as "other."

While collective folly may be an enduring characteristic of the human experience, we do not believe it is the destiny of any particular group. By understanding our propensity for collective folly, and learning how to anticipate and effectively address its consequences, we believe groups and larger collectives can strengthen their potential for collective wisdom.

Just as groups can increase the likelihood of wisdom emerging, by continually tending to the commitments and convictions that allow collective wisdom to arise, they can decrease the likelihood that folly will emerge, through a similar discipline and mindfulness. Such mindfulness begins with awareness that collective folly is a potential of *every* group, it can emerge among us at any time in any context, and it has almost limitless manifestations.

THE TWO MOVEMENTS OF
COLLECTIVE FOLLY

Underneath its many forms, however, are at least two funda-mental patterns that, when recognized, can alert us to the po-tential of folly's emergence. The first pattern is a movement toward separation and fragmentation. In this pattern, group members resist ideas, other group members, or other groups that are deemed "not me" or "not us." Sometimes this pull is subtle. Group members ignore divergent perspectives or data, welcoming only the data and perspectives that confirm what we know, or think we know. The cognitive sciences describe this behavior as *confirmation bias*—a tendency to search for and interpret information in ways that confirm our existing pre-conceptions. Anything different from what we know is "not us" and therefore is consciously or unconsciously excluded.

At other times, this pull toward separation and fragmen-tation is stronger, dragging us toward polarization. When caught in this more powerful pull toward folly, we actively declare as "other" any ideas or people who contradict our beliefs. Instead of seeking to understand and integrate di-vergent ideas, we reject them, declaring them "heretical" or "dangerous." Instead of acting to build relationships and deeper trust with people who disagree with us, we call them "deluded" or "selfish" or "evil." At its most extreme, this movement declares other groups as not-human, or of such threat to "us" that all forms of exclusion, including violence, are justified.

However subtle or extreme, the direction of collective folly's first movement is the same: away from wisdom's deeper connections and more expansive understandings, toward more fearful separation and fragmentation.

The second pattern of collective folly is the mirror image of the first: Rather than a movement toward separation and fragmentation, this is a movement toward false agreement and the appearance of unity. In this movement, group members choose silence and conformity, preferring to preserve an illusion of collective coherence rather than revealing the divergence within the group. This movement masks a separation that *already exists* and, consequently, prevents the group from considering data and perspectives that could help it develop a more complete understanding of the reality it faces. Like the first pattern, this pattern is also a movement away from wisdom's deeper connections and more expansive understandings, but here an existing separation and fragmentation is fearfully preserved in the form of false agreement. These two movements—toward fragmentation and separation on the one hand, toward false coherence on the other—recur repeatedly in experiences of collective folly.

Collective wisdom is not simply a celebration of the positive aspects of groups. It invites us to consider the difference between behaviors that deepen our awareness and those that lead us into the trap of collective folly. In these next stories, we seek to illuminate some of these patterns, revealing the often-tragic consequences that occur when groups are not alert to their ever-present potential for falling into the trap.

"P R O V I N G" W H A T W E K N O W

Some people say that the Wise Men of Helm are fools. Don't you believe it. It's just that foolish things are always happening to them.

—Solomon Simon, *The Wise Men of Helm and Their Merry Tales*

Sometimes humor and fable can help us get enough distance from human behavior to see ourselves and our patterns more clearly. In the 1940s, Solomon Simon wrote a series of fables about the town of Helm, a curious place hidden deep in the mountainous forests of Eastern Europe.[1] The oral tradition of these tales dates back to at least the 1500s. No one knows exactly how Helm came to be, Simon wrote, but one origin tale has it that an angel was carrying a sackful of foolish souls back up to heaven for mending when he got lost in a storm. As the angel struggled to find his way, his sack got caught on the point of a tall tree, ripped, and spilled all of the foolish souls down the mountainside into Helm. Another origin tale had it that a strange stream of air, known for making human beings into simpletons, blew into Helm one day, and the Helmites breathed so deeply that they, their children, and their children's children were afflicted.

However Helm came to be, what is most notable about the town, according to Simon, is that people there seem to reason . . . um . . . *differently* from the way people in other parts of the world do (or at least think we do). For example, the town sages often busy themselves by testing the logical reasoning of young novices. One novice might be asked a chemistry question: "What sweetens a glass of tea: the sugar or the teaspoon that stirs it?" If you answered, "The sugar, of course!" you would not make it far in the town of Helm. The right answer in Helm is that the teaspoon sweetens the tea; the sugar is needed only to tell the stirrer when to stop stirring. When the sugar has dissolved, the person can stop stirring, confident that the spoon has been in the tea long enough to sweeten it.

Another novice might be asked: "What makes the oceans salty?" "Herring" is the right answer in Helm. Since the herring eaten in Helm are salted, when they swim in the ocean, they must make the water salty. Still another novice might be asked a meteorology question: "Why are summer days long and winter days short?" In Helm, everyone knows that heat expands and cold contracts. Therefore, summer days expand because of the heat, and winter days contract because of the cold. What could be more obvious?

Indeed.

As Simon retells and weaves anew the stories of Helm, the reader begins to see patterns of misguided thinking, faulty logic, and confirmation bias. To test the hypothesis that the spoon sweetens the tea and not the sugar, for example, we might try to sweeten the tea using the same spoon but with no sugar, or the same spoon with salt instead of sugar, and compare the results. Convinced that the teaspoon sweetens the tea, however, we do not explore data that might challenge this preconception; instead we create a spurious rationale for the sugar, namely that it is needed to measure the time required by the spoon to stir the tea.

And lest we think that such faulty reasoning occurs only in fables, one of the developing story lines about the United States government's 2003 decision to go to war in Iraq is about confirmation bias. George Tenet, CIA director during the years leading to the war, wrote a book in 2007 titled *At the Center of the Storm*. As reported in the *New York Times*:

> Mr. Tenet takes blame for the flawed 2002 National Intelligence Estimate about Iraq's weapons programs, calling the episode "one of the lowest moments of my seven-year tenure." He expresses regret that the document was not more nuanced, but says there was no doubt in his mind at the time that Saddam Hussein possessed unconventional weapons. "In retrospect, we got it wrong partly because the truth was so implausible," he writes.[2]

If we are convinced that something is true—Saddam Hussein has unconventional weapons—then, under the spell of confirmation bias, we look only for data that confirms our bias and reject or interpret away any data that might challenge what we already know to be true.

This tendency in human beings, and human beings in groups—to seek only data that confirms what we already believe to be true—underscores the importance of the stances we discussed earlier, such as the commitment to seeing whole systems/seeking diverse perspectives and the need to suspend certainty. These stances prepare us to welcome divergence, not fear it, and encourage us to seek out data that may challenge our current perspectives, allowing us a more nuanced view of reality.

A more perplexing dimension of life in Helm—at least for a book about collective wisdom—is that nothing of import is done without deep thought and extended group discussions. It is not unusual for Helm's sages and leading citizens to gather for seven days and seven nights when the town faces a particularly complex issue, considering all possibilities before they arrive at their best solution.

One year, a crisis involving dangerous falls from a high cliff brings the whole community together. Something must be done. A number of young children who play in the field near the cliff have fallen and been seriously injured. What to do? For seven days and seven nights the townspeople meet together and discuss the situation. Nothing is more important in Helm than the safety of the children. They examine option after option: Perhaps the field should be off-limits to children under a certain age; maybe adults should always be present to monitor the children's activities; or maybe the town should build fences at the edge of the field to prevent the falls. All of these options are discussed at length, and all are found wanting. Finally, after days of discussion, the group hits upon an idea that everyone agrees is the best: The town will build a hospital at the bottom of the cliff. This way, when the children fall, the town will be able to tend to their injuries faster. All agree: This is the best possible solution, and so it is that a hospital is built at the bottom of the cliff.

Uh-huh.

After days of group discussion, this is the solution? Collective folly indeed. Treating the children's injuries is important, of course, but doesn't the town want to address the causes of the problem rather than simply getting better at responding to its consequences? Further reflection renders the story even more agitating. The townspeople have such good intentions; they want to do right by their children. From the perspective of collective wisdom, the story offers a clear warning that good intentions and extensive group interactions may not by themselves be sufficient to help groups avoid the dangers of faulty logic, confirmation bias, or just bad decisions.

PROTECTING "US" BY ATTACKING AN "OTHER"

This last story about the Helmites begins to suggest another source of collective folly. In many of Simon's tales of Helm, the town sages do not know that they do not know. They do not consciously repress the contrary perspective or divergent data; it is simply inconceivable to them, much as the possibility that Saddam Hussein did not have weapons of mass destruction was implausible to George Tenet.

In this last story, however, the town gathers and discusses lots of options. No option seems to be intentionally excluded, but in the end, the option they choose will do nothing to solve the problem they face. How is this possible?

One of the active group dynamics among Helmites is that, whatever else they may be, they know that they are *not* fools. Foolish things may *happen* to them, but they are not fools; they are wise men and women. Everyone else, in all of the surrounding villages, is a fool, but the people of Helm are wise. This belief in their inherent wisdom is an essential part of the Helmites' identity as a group. Since they are not fools, they cannot make foolish decisions; therefore, any decision they reach must be wise, must be the right decision. *And so it is that a hospital is built at the bottom of the cliff.*

The people of Helm are blind to their capacity for foolishness. We call this part of a group's behavior or identity that the group itself cannot see *collective shadow*. Psychologists use the term *shadow* to refer to those parts of our identity that an individual or group rejects. Unable or unwilling to acknowledge less positive motives or drives as "of us," we often project them out onto others or the larger world.

In 1973, the Jewish writer Isaac Bashevis Singer, who won the Nobel Prize in Literature five years later, updated the Helm stories, focusing on this darker potentiality of collective shadow and projection. In our recounting of Singer's tale, Helm is ruled by a Council of Sages. When the tale opens, no longer are these sages instructing novices on the sweetness of tea or the differences in the seasons.[3]

THE HEAD SAGE IS GRONAM Ox, and he has called the Council of Sages together because Helm faces a crisis. Many of the people of Helm live in poverty: They lack enough bread to eat, they dress in rags, and illness is common. After seven days and nights of individual contemplation, the sages gather to explore possible responses.

One sage observes that most people in Helm are not educated enough to know what the word *crisis* means. He recommends passing a law forbidding the use of the word. Without the word, no one in Helm will know there is a crisis. Problem solved. Another sage has a different approach: Pass a law requiring two days of fasting per week for every person in Helm. No more bread shortage.

But what about the shortage of clothes? Easy, says a third sage. "If we tax shoes, boots, and other common articles of clothing, then the poor will not be able to afford them. This will leave more clothes for the rich. Who cares about the poor, anyway?"

"I do!" exclaims a fourth sage. "We need the poor to work in the factories and the fields. So let the poor break into the houses of the rich at night and steal the clothes they need. Then they will be able to work in the fields and the factories without getting sick. Who cares about the rich?"

"This will never work," says another sage. "There are far more poor people than rich people. The poor will never be able to steal enough to meet their needs. We should outlaw clothes, so that all in Helm walk around naked. No clothes, no more clothes shortage."

And on it goes, as each proposed solution is met with an equally compelling counterargument. It appears that nothing will be decided. The usual solution at these times is to postpone the discussion until a future meeting, thus allowing the sages to spend more time in contemplation. On this occasion, however, Gronam Ox has a different idea. To meet this extraordinary crisis, Gronam Ox proposes an extraordinary solution: war. Only a war can save the village. What? How? Why? Who? the sages cry out. They don't have an army, they don't have an enemy, and they don't have a reason. Gronam Ox remains calm. Helm will declare war on the town of Gorshkov.

Why Gorshkov? "Because the people in Gorshkov call us fools!" The way to show them that the people of Helm are not fools is to defeat them in war. And though the people of Gorshkov are even poorer than those in Helm, they can be enslaved and made to do the work necessary to maintain Helm.

But what about an army, and weapons? Gronam Ox has an answer for this too. They will forge weapons from the pots and pans that are no longer needed because of the food shortage. They will raise an army from the young who are idle because there are no jobs. Our course is clear! Gronam Ox declares with authority. Helm will forge weapons, assemble an army, and launch a surprise attack on Gorshkov in the dead of night. Helm will be victorious, and all will again be well.

The sages are euphoric. One declares Gronam Ox the greatest sage, not only of Helm, but of the whole world. Others suggest that Gronam Ox be made emperor and that castles be built for him. After much celebration, one of the sages is recognized to speak. He has a few nagging questions: For instance, how will Helm's army get to Gorshkov in the dead of night, since there are no roads between the two towns? And how will the army get beyond the locked gate and wall that surrounds Gorshkov? The other sages are stunned—how could he ask such questions?—and quickly shout their colleague down, calling him a traitor and threatening to hang him. So much for welcoming divergence. Having achieved such a clear "consensus," the council adjourns.

Of course, nothing goes as planned. First, Yenta Pesha, Gronam Ox's wife, objects to giving up her pots and pans to be made into weapons. "We have enough trouble without a war!" she cries, but to no avail. Young men are recruited for the army, and since there are fewer people to work the fields now, the harvest is even more meager than it had been in previous years. No matter. The town is preparing for war. The autumn rains come, and since none of the soldiers have shoes or decent coats, most catch colds. Still, the town is preparing for war; Helmites will just have to make do.

Finally, Gronam Ox declares that the night has come to attack Gorshkov. The army promptly gets lost and ends up at the wrong village. They are outside Mazelborsht, not Gorshkov. No problem. Gronam Ox decides that the army should attack this new "enemy." After all, there are also people in Mazelborsht who think Helmites are fools. The night's journey, however, has taken its toll on the soldiers. Exhausted and sick, they quickly flee when the villagers of Mazelborsht fight back. The Helm army returns to their village defeated. Having prepared for a joyous celebration, the townspeople now weep with the news of their defeat.

Gronam Ox convenes the sages for another emergency session. They are ready to learn from their experience of war. After seven days and seven nights, they come together and make several vital decisions. First, they declare that Gronam Ox is still the exalted leader and sage of sages of Helm. Second, they decide that in the future, they will use spies to better assess their enemies. They also decide that Helm's army will no longer use pestles for weapons, presumably because these did not work so well against Mazelborsht.

In this revised tale of Helm, Singer reveals the darker dimensions of a polarizing stance that declares "not us." In the earlier tales, Helmites simply ignored the divergent perspective: Since it is the teaspoon that sweetens the tea, the sugar must be there simply to mark the time needed for stirring. In Singer's tale, the sages' first responses to the poverty crisis demonstrate that ignoring the divergent is still in their repertoire. Outlaw the use of the word *crisis*; then nobody will know there is one. But then a more sinister movement arises, a polarizing movement to create an "other." The first manifestation of this movement separates Helmites into rich and poor. Tax the poor so that the rich will have more. Who cares about the poor, anyway? No, let the poor rob from the rich. Who cares about the rich?

Collective folly often has its roots in some form of anxiety—a "crisis" of material, emotional, or spiritual origins—that induces a movement to separate, to fragment. The word *crisis* comes in part from the Greek word *krinein*, meaning "to separate," and we see that one of the first responses to the crisis in Helm is to separate rich from poor so that one will benefit and the other will pay. In times of crisis, we can become anxious, confused, and unsure what to do. In these moments, we can easily project our fears outward, searching for someone or some group to blame or punish. "Stick it to the poor!" "No, stick it to the rich!"

The euphoric response to Gronam Ox's solution suggests that he has tapped into something deep within the other sages. By declaring that they will go to war, Gronam shifts the focus of the separation movement: It's not rich Helmites against poor Helmites; it is *all* Helmites against the condescending Gorshkovites. The problem is not with any of *us*; it's with *them*, the Gorshkovites. Not only is the problem not *us*, but now we have a lot to do. We have weapons to make, an army to raise, and attack plans to finalize. Indeed, as the Helmites prepare for war, the original conditions that gave rise to this plan actually get worse: The harvest is smaller, and more people are sick. But how can we talk about these things now when there is a war upon us?

As anxiety and fear rise within groups, the pressure to *do something* can become unbearable: Anything is better than sitting with the anxiety of feeling stuck or lost, of not knowing. Collective wisdom invites a group to embrace not knowing, and to trust that a deeper wisdom will emerge as the group welcomes the divergent and works to include the dissonance that may be present in its social field.

Groups that cannot hold such ambiguity become more susceptible to folly arising. The possibility of a savior, or a saving idea, becomes even more seductive at these moments; and once a group has identified with its savior, it can be brutal in repressing what it perceives as resistance. This is why the sage who asks the nagging questions is immediately branded a traitor and threatened with hanging. The movement toward separation grows more violent, even before the war. So relieved is the group to have a way forward, any way forward, that they threaten one of their own with expulsion and death.

In moments of collective folly arising, the exterior movement of separation—the creation of an "other" among us or outside of us—often mirrors an interior movement of separation. The group can experience a separation from its own inner knowing as fears and anxieties arise. What we want is certainty, certainty that we know what to do, or at least whom to blame; and when the doubts and questions arise within us, we repress them in ourselves or repress them in the group. The space to imagine different possibilities collapses; only certain feelings and thoughts are permissible. No inquiry here; we have the answer that will solve our problems and allay our fears.

This movement of separation not only can pit group against group; it can also pit group member against group member. Sometimes this group conflict emerges because a member of the group asks a question, takes a position, or behaves in a way that threatens the group's perception of itself, as one sage did when he raised questions about Gronam Ox's plan to go to war. His questions raised the possibility that the plan was not well conceived, which might imply that the plan and its endorsers were foolish—"Traitor! Hang him!"

When the individual asking the questions also views his accusers as "others," the intragroup conflict can degenerate into intractable polarization, leading to results that *no one* wants. Often the results are tragic, as the following story of childbed fever illustrates.

five

The Tragedy of Polarized Groups

gnaz Semmelweis (pronounced "Eeg-natz Shemmel-vise") is a well-known figure in medical history. Some twenty years before the work of Louis Pasteur, Joseph Lister, and others substantiated a germ theory of disease, and Lister recommended an antiseptic practice of surgery, Semmelweis discovered how simple hand-washing techniques could dramatically reduce the fatal incidence of childbed fever in new mothers.[1]

CHILDBED FEVER WAS RAMPANT in Europe in 1844 when Semmelweis graduated from the Vienna Medical School. Although many births still occurred at home, increasing numbers of mothers were going to hospitals to deliver their babies. Hospitals routinely reported deaths due to childbed fever of as many as 25 percent of all women giving birth, and sometimes up to 100 percent. No one understood why. There were a number of competing theories. One was that childbed fever was like smallpox, a specific disease with a unique cause, and that it came and went in epidemics. Another theory was that it was caused by a miasma, a poisonous mist or cloud that the Greeks and others had invoked to explain otherwise-inexplicable diseases. Many in the medical profession at the time believed that the cholera epidemic was caused by a miasma.

Upon graduating from medical school, Semmelweis became an assistant to Johann Klein, professor of obstetrics at the Vienna Medical School. In this position, Semmelweis oversaw one of two obstetrics divisions of Vienna General Hospital. Shortly after assuming his position, he became obsessed with childbed fever. Over the next several years, he compiled data that might help him develop an answer for why so many mothers were dying.

One of the first things Semmelweis did was to compare the results from the two obstetrics divisions. What he discovered mystified him. In his division, an average of six hundred to eight hundred mothers died each year; in the other division, the number was sixty: one-tenth as many. This was particularly puzzling to him, because both divisions delivered the same number of babies—about thirty-five hundred each year—and were the same in all other discernible ways except one: In Semmelweis's division, only doctors and medical students delivered babies; in the other division, only midwives did.

Through his research, he also found that even when deaths were high in his clinic, there was not a corresponding spike in childbed deaths outside in the city of Vienna. Mortality rates among mothers who delivered their babies at home remained consistently low. Had there been an epidemic of childbed fever, it would be reasonable to assume that mothers delivering at home would also "catch" the disease, but the data showed otherwise. These and other observations led him to reject the epidemic and miasma theories, and to hypothesize that something must be happening in his division that was different from what occurred in the other division.

INDIVIDUAL WISDOM, COLLECTIVE FOLLY

It was now 1847. Semmelweis had been painstakingly compiling his data for almost three years. His father had died in the previous year, and now, without warning, an admired professor and mentor died suddenly. Semmelweis was distraught. How could this have happened? He pored over the records of his professor's death, trying to make some sense of why his mentor died. What he learned was that the doctor had cut himself during an autopsy and died shortly thereafter from a virulent infection in the wound. Semmelweis had a sudden flash of insight. The rapid deterioration and death of his professor looked exactly like the deaths of the mothers in his division. Since his mentor had died from an infection caused by his wound coming in contact with a cadaver, could the same be true for the mothers who were dying?

Semmelweis concluded that the answer was yes. It was common practice for students and doctors to go to the delivery wards just after completing autopsies for research or classroom studies. Sanitary conditions were primitive, and physicians sometimes did not even wash their hands between autopsy and delivery. If they were carrying invisible particles of infection from the cadavers (or from any other source) on their hands when they began to assist with the mother's delivery, then they could be introducing into the mother's body the infection that would kill her. This would also explain the discrepancy in deaths between the two divisions: midwives did not do autopsies.

To test his hypothesis, Semmelweis ordered doctors and students in his division to adopt a hand-washing technique employing a chlorine solution before they delivered any baby. This solution had proved effective at removing the smell of the cadaver from a doctor's hands, a telling indication of what Semmelweis called "invisible cadaver particles." The change had an immediate impact. In 1848, the first full year after the hand-washing technique was applied, deaths in Semmelweis's division fell dramatically, coming in line with rates from the other division and rates reported for home births.

Semmelweis had made a breakthrough discovery. While he had not yet developed a theoretical justification for his insight, he had persuasive results. Before the hand-washing technique, there had been over six hundred deaths in his division; after the hand-washing technique, forty-five. For next to nothing, hospitals across Europe and elsewhere could easily adopt this procedure and save literally thousands of women's lives each year.

Thousands of lives saved for little or no expense, by instituting a simple hand-washing procedure—what could be simpler? Give the doctor some awards, fund an expansion of his research, teach his techniques around the world, and celebrate. Right?

Wrong. There were no celebrations. In fact, within a year of his discovery, Semmelweis was rejected for reappointment to his position in the medical school. Even worse, his division discontinued the hand-washing practice after he left, and the mortality rate among mothers returned to their much-higher rates. It would be almost twenty years before Pasteur showed how bacteria—Semmelweis's "invisible cadaver particles"—caused putrefaction in dead bodies and hospitals began to adopt the practical strategies for minimizing infection recommended by Lister and his peers.

Twenty years. Tens of thousands of mothers dead. Why?

The reasons are complicated, and have been explored in myriad medical histories and biographies. At the heart of this story, however, are telltale movements of separation and fragmentation, of polarization and shadow, within the medical establishment in Vienna and within Semmelweis himself.

POLARIZATION IS A WOUND OF THE COLLECTIVE BODY

Semmelweis's theory did not simply challenge the prevailing medical theories about the causes of childbed fever; it challenged a deeply held identity structure of the medical establishment. While there were several theories about childbed fever—it was a unique disease like smallpox, it was the result of a miasma, it was the result of an imbalance in the four humors of the body—what was common among these disparate theories was a simple but ultimately lethal assumption: Whatever was causing childbed fever, it was not the *doctors* who were at fault. They were committed healers doing everything they could for their patients. They grieved with each mother's death. Something mysterious, beyond human comprehension and responsibility, must be at work. To accept Semmelweis's theory would require long-practicing obstetricians to acknowledge that, however unwittingly, they had been the instrument of their patients' deaths.

We are back in Helm, without the humor: The doctors saw themselves as committed professionals, as caring healers; it was unfathomable to them that they could be the cause of their patients' deaths. Therefore, anyone who would suggest such a thing must be (fill in the blank): deluded, misguided, naïve, dangerous, treacherous, evil. Semmelweis was called all of these things and more.

The doctors who rejected Semmelweis's theory, and ultimately moved to expel him from the medical school, had other reasons as well. Even before Semmelweis's discovery, the medical school was polarized between older and younger faculty members. Vienna in the 1840s was the political and cultural center of the Hapsburg Empire. Conflicts festered throughout the empire and Europe, presaging the multiple (and mostly failed) revolutions that erupted across Europe in 1848. The Austrian government controlled most of the empire's institutions, including the University of Vienna and its medical school. Many of the older professors owed their positions to their allegiance to government leaders. Many of the younger medical school faculty members chafed at the support that the older professors received from the government. They also resented the older doctors' adherence to medical orthodoxies: Many younger faculty members were exploring new research methodologies and new theories of disease causation, which were often resisted if not ridiculed by their older colleagues.

Polarization is a form of group wound that, left untreated, can infect the entire collective body. As each side seeks to inflict harm on the other, members are often unaware that the resulting wounds are weakening the entire body, not just "the other." When Semmelweis articulated a new theory of disease causation that appeared to prove the medical establishment *wrong*, other younger faculty members rejoiced. This was not just about mothers dying needlessly; this was about academic freedom and a new world order. Time to attack.

And who was one of the chief leaders of the old guard who came under attack? Johann Klein, professor of obstetrics and Semmelweis's supervisor. It was in the midst of this and the broader cultural turmoil of 1848 that Semmelweis's appointment came up for renewal. Instead of Semmelweis, Klein chose a new candidate for the position, who, like Klein, rejected Semmelweis's theory and methods.

Unable to accept that they could be instruments of their patients' dying, critical and perhaps fearful of what the younger faculty members intended, and committed to maintain both their positions and their reputations, Klein and his peers had many conscious and unconscious reasons for rejecting Semmelweis and his proposals. In medical conferences, journals, and the popular press, they challenged his methods, the accuracy of his data, and his lack of a theoretical framework to explain his results. The call from many in the medical establishment was to banish Semmelweis and his ideas from the community.

PERSONALIZING THE SYSTEM'S DYSFUNCTION

Tragically, this may have been just the result that Semmelweis was seeking, at least unconsciously. After he made such a compelling discovery, the obvious next step would have been for him to carefully document his clinical findings and publish them in various medical journals. This was, and still is, the well-established way to introduce the medical and scientific communities to breakthrough research, particularly research that challenges existing understanding and practice. A number of doctors had expressed interest in Semmelweis's work when some of his colleagues lectured or wrote about it. Some began testing his recommended practices but did not get the results that Semmelweis claimed. Later research would identify the need for strict enforcement of the hand-washing procedure. Semmelweis himself had to create such controls to ensure that doctors and students were properly using the recommended chlorine wash.

Despite this interest, however, and despite encouragement from many of his supporters, Semmelweis chose not to publish his research. Instead, he bristled at the questioning of his research and results, calling the skeptics murderers and accusing them of willingly killing innocent women.

Why would he do this? Why would Semmelweis make personal attacks against other doctors, most of whom no doubt cared deeply about their patients and the quality of their care? Why would he not take the simple path of documenting his research?

One answer may be that, in the highly polarized medical community, it was hard for Semmelweis to distinguish between questions that were motivated by honest inquiry and questions that were masks for an attack to discredit him. In a highly polarized group, motives are often suspect; any interaction can quickly become an opportunity for attack, one side seeking to bolster its positions and undermine the credibility of the other.

While Semmelweis may have harbored such fears, the story is more complex. At least one biographer, Sherwin Nuland, suggests that Semmelweis's actions during this time reveal an identity structure rooted in extreme feelings of unworthiness and of being an outsider. There are many reasons why he may have internalized such feelings. He was born in Hungary, the son of a grocer from a minority tribe. He grew up speaking an odd German dialect, not learning Hungarian until secondary school. His language and his accent would have marked him as an outsider, both in Hungary and in Vienna, where Hungarians were often viewed as foreigners and second-class citizens. After graduating from medical school, he was rejected for positions in forensic pathology and medicine before settling for a position in obstetrics, a field where midwives, nondoctors, still dominated the practice.

To speculate about another's interior reality is always risky; we can never fully know how Semmelweis saw himself or why. What we can reflect upon is his behavior and what that behavior *might* suggest about his interior reality. If someone has feelings of unworthiness that he cannot acknowledge and integrate within himself, these feelings can become suppressed and acted out in destructive ways. With such a person, the theory of shadow and projection would predict that he would find himself constantly in conflict with people he perceived as ignorant and inferior, as he projected his subconscious feelings onto others. And if this person's suppressed feelings of unworthiness were tied to an unconscious identification with being an "outsider," it would not be surprising if the person acted in ways that ensured that he *became* an outsider.

This is exactly what Semmelweis did. To say that he was a polarizing personality would be kind. As Nuland observes, reflecting on a series of handwritten letters by Semmelweis attacking his detractors, "He was a hellfire-spewing evangelist and an afflicter of conscience all at once, the kind of righteous goad that no one wants to be near. More than one obstetrician who might otherwise have been favorably disposed to giving his techniques a fair trial was put off by [his] abrasive manner in which he attempted to make them dip and drink at his antiseptic trough of truth."[2] Time after time, when Semmelweis had an opportunity to secure acceptance for himself and his ideas, he acted in ways that virtually guaranteed opposition and resistance. Rather than seeking ways to honor the whole, to stay in relationship with his community and invite deeper reflection, Semmelweis personalized the conflict and inflamed it further.

Klein and his allies in the medical school rejected Semmelweis, in part because of their inability to hold the possibility that they could be complicit in the deaths of their patients. Semmelweis attacked Klein and many others in the Vienna medical community, making it much more likely that he would be ostracized. Projection is hurled against projection, attack is met with counterattack, the polarization metastasizes . . . and tens of thousands of people die.

Could the medical school community have chosen a different way? Was a different way possible? From within the fog of polarization, it can be hard to see any other way but conflict. And once in that fog, confirmation bias further blinds us, as we interpret every event in light of what we already "know": namely that "they" are attacking "us."

six

An Illusion of Agreement

The stories of Helm and of childbed fever bear witness to the tragic consequences that can emerge from collective folly's movement toward separation and fragmentation. Tragedy can also ensue from the second movement of collective folly, toward the illusion of agreement and unity. While the emergence of collective wisdom is often signaled by an enveloping silence of deeper knowing and connection, the emergence of collective folly is often signaled by a different kind of silence, an agitated silence where words are suppressed in fear or resignation. Such silences can give the appearance of cohesion but often mask dramatic divisions that permeate the group. When groups act from this false belief in agreement, almost always they have merely postponed the conflict until a later date, and often the false front leads to tragic results.

In the documentary *In the Shadow of the Moon*, Apollo astronaut John Young recalled a conversation about a safety concern he had had with Lieutenant Colonel Virgil I. "Gus" Grissom, a friend and colleague he had known since his earliest days at NASA. They had flown together in the first manned Gemini flight in 1965. "I couldn't believe it," Young recalled. "He said, 'I can't say anything about it or they'll fire me.'"[1]

Grissom was scheduled to be the command pilot of the first manned Apollo launch into outer space. Young had asked Grissom about the dangers from the nest of electrical wiring in the Apollo capsule, and Grissom went silent. He didn't want to talk about it. Two weeks later, on January 27, 1967, during a routine training on emergency procedures, a spark of unknown origin ignited the command module, incinerating Grissom and his two fellow astronauts.

Why would Grissom, a decorated Air Force pilot and one of the original Project Mercury astronauts, hesitate to speak up about his concerns?

This is a particularly troubling question because, unlike the doctors in our story of the Vienna medical school, participants in the Apollo program describe a team full of good will and cooperation. Inventing a spacecraft to transport human beings safely to the moon and back was a mind-bogglingly complex undertaking. Project managers divided the tasks of designing the rocket and its capsule into teams, each team comprising astronauts, engineers, managers, and other experts. The teams were highly motivated, with members working side by side to solve their part of the design equation. It is hard to imagine a brighter, more dedicated, more loyal group of people joined together for a purpose that was personally and collectively valued. And Gus Grissom was no Semmelweis: By all accounts, he was respected and well liked. Many predicted he would be the first astronaut to step onto the moon. If Grissom could be silenced, it could happen to any of us. In any group. At any time.

There are times when we need to be heard and the pressures of group life mute our speech. There are also times when the systems we have designed become so complicated and so daunting that no one individual feels capable of effecting change. While we cannot see or touch "resistance," "fragmentation," or "fear," we know the feeling of not being heard, of being cut short, or of being told we are wrong or worse. Sometimes in groups we lose our capacity to listen carefully to each other, to hear "between the words" and to recognize and engage hesitation and caution. In these moments, the space for inquiry collapses, and as a result, we are all in danger. (Depth psychology has long pointed out that what individuals do not see and resolve in themselves will appear as a negative fate. We can apply this insight to groups as well and say that what the group cannot or will not see of its own behavior reveals itself later in some form of collective tragedy.)

We cannot know what Grissom meant when he described his reluctance to speak out about the wiring hazards.

Perhaps he was referring to a specific conflict with someone who had the power to scratch him from the mission. Maybe he had just given up, finally succumbing to the cumulative frustrations of trying to get others to pay attention to complex questions they repeatedly dismissed. It is easy to imagine, given the pressures and complexity of the task, that many conversations went wanting simply for lack of time and too many other contingencies to tend to, rather than for any ill will or intentional ignorance. The potential lethal hazards were myriad, including flammable materials, various wiring problems, plumbing flaws, and a hatch that might not open in an emergency. What we can say is that Grissom's comment "I can't say anything about it or they'll fire me" pointed to some form of collapse of genuine engagement and collective inquiry.

A NEXT ITERATION: THE EXPLOSION OF THE SPACE SHUTTLE CHALLENGER

Nineteen years later, tragedy struck NASA again. On the morning of January 28, 1986, Roger Boisjoly (pronounced "Boy-shzo-lay") sat in a Morton Thiokol conference room watching the launch of the space shuttle *Challenger*. Morton Thiokol was the NASA contractor for rocket boosters, and Boisjoly was the lead for one of the senior engineering teams.[2]

One minute after the launch, one of Boisjoly's team members, Bob Ebeling, whispered that he had just said a prayer of thanks for a safe launch. Thirteen seconds later, the shuttle disintegrated in a fiery explosion that killed all seven crew members. Everyone in the conference room fell silent, stunned at what they had just witnessed.

Boisjoly walked back to his office distraught, unable to speak. He was horrified by what had just happened, but not surprised. He had been warning his superiors for months about the risks related to the O-ring seals used on the booster rockets. One day earlier, on the anniversary of the *Apollo I* disaster, he had finally persuaded senior management to recommend a "no launch." His entire seal task team had unanimously agreed; there should not be a flight on January 28. But the launch proceeded as scheduled. What happened?

What happened was a tragedy, again made more puzzling by the absence of any ill intention. The people involved did not mean harm. Had someone asked, all would have affirmed that the astronauts' safety was their paramount concern. Nevertheless, a collective field of silence or suppression, echoing in an almost eerie way Young's memory of Grissom's comment, was suggested by the disaster. In this case, however, we have far more information.

THE UNCOMFORTABLE CONVERSATION THAT GUS Grissom never had, or had given up on, was taken up by Boisjoly the day before the launch in a conference call with thirty-three other key members from Morton Thiokol and NASA officials. NASA officials organized the call to review the surprise recommendation by Morton Thiokol to cancel the launch. Although Boisjoly had written memos and spoken to Morton Thiokol managers about the O-ring seals, his concerns had not been shared with NASA. During the call, Boisjoly could now talk directly to NASA about his fears. Boisjoly's team shared with NASA its data about seal resiliency in colder weather. They warned NASA officials that the seals might fail in temperatures below 53 degrees Fahrenheit. The overnight forecast at the launch site was 18 degrees.

A senior NASA official, Larry Mulloy, took charge of the call. He reviewed the data that Boisjoly and the other engineers had presented, and declared it inconclusive. The engineers admitted that they did not have definitive data on O-ring performance in the temperature predicted for the next day's launch, 29 degrees. In one case, O-ring erosion had occurred when it was 70 degrees outside. Could the engineers be sure there was even a correlation between low temperatures and erosion? The launch had already been delayed four times, and a new delay could set them back months. Was Morton Thiokol really prepared to recommend a no-launch decision?

Mulloy then asked George Hardy, NASA's deputy director of science and engineering, for his response to the no-launch recommendation. Hardy said that he was "appalled" at the recommendation coming now, on the eve of the launch, but he would not launch over the contractor's objections.

At this point, a senior manager at Morton Thiokol requested to go off-line in order to reevaluate their recommendation. When the mute button was pushed, Jerry Mason, Morton Thiokol's general manager, spoke: "We have to make a management decision." Boisjoly knew what this meant. It was time for the engineers to shut up. But they didn't shut up. First one and then another argued for a no-launch decision. At one point, Boisjoly grabbed the photographs showing evidence of the seal failure and forcefully put them in front of the managers. "Look at these photographs. Look at what they are telling us."

The senior managers were conflicted. The conversation continued, and then Mason spoke again. "Am I the only one who wants to fly?" He turned to the vice president of engineering and asked him to take off his engineering hat and put on his management hat. No one had to say what this meant. NASA was one of the firm's most important clients, and its executives expected Morton Thiokol to know what it was doing. Did they know what they were doing? Hadn't they planned for margins of error, hadn't they installed secondary seal systems to prevent exactly this kind of seal failure? These were not questions of inquiry; they were more like accusations. The heat of the moment began to burn through the conversation's internal logic and the group's values concerning safety. The space for genuine engagement and inquiry was collapsing.

Thirty minutes into the conversation, Mason asked for a vote on the recommendation, but only from the senior managers. The engineers were not polled. All four managers voted to launch. One of the managers wrote down the case for the launch on a notepad and then took the phone off mute. The Morton Thiokol executives reported that they were now recommending a "go" for launch. There were grounds for concern, they acknowledged, but the data was inconclusive. Over the speakerphone, a NASA executive asked if anyone had a different position.

Silence.

Treatises on leadership frequently extol the value of individual moral courage to speak up, to act in spite of the group, which is exactly what Boisjoly and his team had done. Boisjoly spoke up, again and again, until finally, silence. Far less often, however, do leadership texts address the group's responsibility to seek out and honor the truths held by individuals, particularly when those truths may be divergent from the group's current thinking. The pressures of group life are immense; rarely does someone want to be the person to say no when the rest of the group wants to say, "Yes already!" and move forward.

As the story of the *Challenger* disaster unfolds, we witness the slow collapsing of the space for inquiry and exploration. In the months prior to the launch, Morton Thiokol executives did not alert senior NASA officials about Boisjoly's concerns, perhaps distracted by other issues, perhaps thinking the data inconclusive, perhaps thinking that the risk of cold temperatures in Florida was not a major concern. When they finally did contact senior NASA officials, it was the day before a launch that had already been delayed four times. NASA officials were angry and dismayed, and said so. This communication was not made between equals, however; Morton Thiokol was a contractor for NASA. NASA wrote the checks. And Mulloy, one of NASA's team members, was questioning Morton Thiokol's competence.

Already small, the room for inquiry, for spacious consideration of doubts and hesitations, grew smaller.

Then the Morton Thiokol team went off-line. The engineers presented the data again and urged delay. But the person with the most power in the room, the general manager, made it clear that he wanted to fly. He stopped engaging the engineers. The movement toward separation became more overt; the space for inquiry grew even smaller. One by one, the other managers came into line, until finally they all "agreed" to support a launch.

The Morton Thiokol executives went back on line. "Our recommendation is a go." The space collapsed altogether. "Does anyone have a different position?" Silence. Roger Boisjoly would later recall that he never even heard the question. The space for questions or dissent within the group was gone.

NOTHING THAT IS HUMAN IS ALIEN TO ME

I am a human being. Nothing that is human is alien to me.

—Terence, a Roman playwright and freed slave

Collective folly is a pull—felt in all groups—drawing us in the opposite direction of wisdom. Rather than moving toward deeper connection with others and larger life forces, we feel dragged toward separation and fragmentation. Rather than opening to the divergent, we cling to the known, or to what we think we know. Rather than seeking connection, we move toward polarization, both in ideas and in relationships. Rather than opening to the divergent with curiosity and a commitment to the whole, we enforce conformity and silence, often putting the group and others at risk.

To feel the impact of collective foolishness and violence, as both victim and perpetrator, has been a defining characteristic of what it means to be human. The immediate and lasting consequences of collective folly affect every human being, generation after generation.

The poet Maya Angelou, when she is lecturing or giving a reading, often recites the lines that begin this section: "I am a human being. Nothing that is human is alien to me." She attributes the lines to a Roman playwright named Publius Terentius Afer, or Terence, as he is more commonly known, and then reveals what many in the audience may not know: that Terence was an African man who was enslaved for years by a Roman senator before the senator chose to release him. The impact of Angelou's revelation is immediate, electric: If someone who has been enslaved can claim the full power of his personhood—I am a *human being*—then that power is available to each and every one of us. Terence may have been a slave, but he was always *free*.

For us, the stories in the early chapters of this book resonate with a similarly joyous vibration: The power of collective wisdom is available to every one of us, in any group or larger collective to which we belong. Our exploration of collective folly, however, reveals the other, far less comforting, implication of Terence's bold claim. If *nothing that is human is alien to me*, then I know the poet *and* the thief, I know the teacher *and* the terrorist, I know the victim *and* the perpetrator—they all are within me. The same is true of any group: We are capable of extraordinary acts of grace and kindness and creativity, and equally extraordinary acts of cruelty and violence. No group is exempt—all that is human is within us.

Paradoxically, groups begin to decrease the likelihood of folly arising as soon as they fully embrace their potential for it. This is not easy; our impulse, as we have seen, can be to reject and deny those parts of us that make us uncomfortable or ashamed. Once we can embrace this potentiality, however, we can begin to address the legacy of collective folly and deepen our capacity for collective wisdom. We see in this shift a positive movement toward collective wisdom and the unlimited potential of groups, communities, and larger collectives.

seven

The Unlimited Cocreative Power of Groups and Communities

We must envision our work as a creative act, more akin to the artistic endeavor than the technical process. This never negates skill and technique. But it does suggest that the wellspring... lies in our moral imagination, which I will define as the capacity to imagine something rooted in the challenges of the real world yet capable of giving birth to that which does not yet exist.

—John Paul Lederach, *The Moral Imagination*

W e know that groups are often the settings for stress, discomfort, and wounding. We are also aware that all too often, we are subject to destructive actions and emotions that can influence our thoughts, affect our biochemistry, and even alter our physical

147

brain. Pick up a newspaper, glance at the Internet, turn on the television, or listen to the radio, and we are immediately drawn into images of raw aggression and conflict. Nor can our workplaces or even families be safe havens from agitation, aggression, and worse. Each of these systems has its own conflicted histories, habitual behaviors, and potential new crises.

Seeking collective wisdom is a conscious attempt to elevate group life from its history of fighting tooth and claw to reach the top of the hierarchy or achieve dominance over others. To make different choices than these, we will need to see the world differently, practice behaviors that bring people together, and allow our new behaviors to be the guide for new learning. This is how individuals learn, and it is the same with groups.

The source of our power lies in the human impulses that move us toward wholeness. These impulses are embedded in universal cultural and religious traditions—for good reason. They give expression to what is most fundamentally sound about human nature: what aids survival, what allows for cooperation, and what fosters our ability to accommodate change in our environments. To be foolish is human, but the capacity to choose between acts leading to folly or to wisdom is a uniquely human gift. What then are some of these human impulses that draw us toward wholeness? How are they hidden amid the cultural and religious traditions we sometimes too glibly think we know? We offer three examples:

- In the Jewish tradition, there is the expression *tikkun olam*, which refers to the need for repair of the world. It is specifically not a religious edict to be followed from obligation, but an understanding that if our creative work is not directed at healing social chaos, we are all in jeopardy.

- The Bantu culture of South Africa has the term *ubuntu*, and in Swahili there is a related term, *umoja*. Together they refer to the interdependence of human beings and the spirit of togetherness that is the goal of collective activity. It is a philosophy of grasping our *together* nature— that what happens to one happens to us all. These terms refer to the power of invoking the spirit of community, human fields of belonging.

- Finally, from the Sufi traditions of the twelfth century comes an understanding that there is an intermediary realm between our sense perceptions and the ethereal plane. It is the place of imagination, where what is and what might be is still to be born. Through the human capacity for imagination, we give birth to new forms, new images, new ways of understanding, and new possibilities. The thirteenth-century Persian poet Rumi gave expression to this human impulse when he wrote, "Chase a deer and end up everywhere."

These sources of human power—creative work, healing, community, and imagination—are the engines of collective wisdom. They are, as Mary Parker Follett told us, ways of engaging in reciprocal relationships with each other, ways of sharing *power with* rather than *power over*. We have the *power with* to harness our human imagination in the service of healthier institutions, new forms of cooperation, and more sophisticated ways of handling conflict. We have the *power with* to heal the social chaos around us.

How, then, shall we proceed? How do we find the support we need to help us during times of uncertainty and challenge? How do we embrace conflict as an opportunity for growth? How do we imagine our creative work as rooted in the challenges of the real world but still unformed? How do we recognize the power and possibility within community?

CREATING FIELDS OF BELONGING

The group is always in process, changing, moving, transforming in the ocean of awareness. Individuals certainly influence a group's consciousness, but in turn, the larger group fields that we participate in influence us all. If the group is in peril, or thinks it is, it will act in certain predictable, mostly defensive ways. If the group operates within a certain range of safety and challenge, it will act with a greater instinct for innovation, from curiosity, and even with a willingness to risk its identity. How can we find ways, or amplify existing ways, to aid a group's health and rejuvenative powers? What more important question is there? Indeed, it is through healthy groups, families, communities, and organizations that we cultivate healthy individuals, who in return contribute their best selves to the group. Healing environments free us from the destructive emotions that can fester in groups and direct our attention to a positive future. Bringing this possibility to group consciousness is an invitation for being, to paraphrase the words of poet David Whyte, the ancestors of our future happiness.

Healing derives from the Old English word *haelan*, the root word for *heal*, *whole*, and *holy*. These interrelated words provide us a clue to positive growth in groups. Healing is a process that aims to make us whole, to unify the discordant chords of life into a larger harmony. It is a sacred process. At its simplest, it is an attempt to do more of those things that bring joy and fewer things that cause pain—to make, in the English novelist George Eliot's words, "life less difficult to each other."

Healing energy invariably brings attention to attitudes and beliefs that limit or further our ability to work with others. Healing impulses draw from us actions that are more congruent with our authentic selves. Healing is not cure, but a better way to live with our wounds and restore a sense of meaning and purpose to our lives. It is the act of overcoming obstacles—the ones in our environment that keep us from being sound in body and spirit, and the ones in our mind that block our path to growth and maturation.

Healing is fundamentally relational. If, for example, we are with people who believe in us and seek the best from us, we will find resources within ourselves that we had not imagined and ways of contributing that had not been foreseen. Healing helps us to become more in tune with the rhythms of life; it allows groups and the individuals within them to achieve a resonance with a higher order of consciousness and complexity.

Collective wisdom occurs most reliably when group members feel both safe and challenged to find what is best in themselves and what is best in the group. Often, this means having to create your own community to support what is seeking to emerge. Invariably, these communities are places that provide both safety for personal vulnerability and freedom to explore. These community networks have a magnetic quality. They attract, arouse, provoke, and draw people together. Their potential is unlimited. "Never doubt," Margaret Mead once stated, "that a small group of thoughtful, committed citizens can change the world."[1] We couldn't agree more. Small groups are the seedbed for transformation in fields as diverse as art, philosophy, politics, humor, music, and literature. Here is one example, drawn from Keith Sawyer's book *Group Genius*.[2]

In 1926, during a time of alienation from many of their colleagues at Oxford University's English Department, C. S. Lewis and J. R. R. Tolkien formed a group with other trusted friends called the Inklings. The name was a pun joining together their secret longing to write in new literary forms and their desire to explore, in Tolkien's words, "vague or half formed intimations and ideas." They met at a local pub, and in the safety of their own company, they created a field of imaginative belonging that allowed them to explore ideas rejected or marginalized in the larger culture of Oxford.

The desire to give attention to these half-formed ideas resulted in group experiments. One was that when a new idea emerged in discussion, group members would each write a chapter elaborating on the idea and then read it out loud to each other. Appreciation and further elaboration followed, bringing out perspectives that none of the group members could have had on their own. Tolkien and Lewis, who had kept their more intimate writings private, now became encouraged to share their poetic and mythic inclinations. It is from this imaginative field of belonging that their major works arose. For Lewis, it was *The Chronicles of Narnia*, and for Tolkien, it was *The Hobbit* and *The Lord of the Rings*. Each of their works explored the contours of safety and challenge in life and the impulse to discover something larger than just oneself. And within each of their tales were lessons that with collaboration comes learning, responsibility, and reward.

Creating fields of belonging involves intentional communities such as the example above. In this case, it formed from a response to alienation and took shape in the form of experimentation, devising a group process that met the members' needs. The group, through its members, gave birth to fictional worlds simultaneously addressing matters of theology, mythology, and the recurring patterns of human conduct. Their imagined worlds created new passageways into the human soul. Within, some might say despite, the context of Oxford's academic solemnity, a free-flowing, joyful conversation emerged. How marvelous. Certainly there are parallels with Emerson and the formation and development of the Transcendentalist Club. Both involved settings where safety was accompanied by creative work and each served the other. Cultivating such settings is akin to weaving a new social fabric that welcomes our diverse human gifts and finds a place for our talents.

A second example. Renee Levi, an organizational consultant, became fascinated with the concept of *collective resonance*—which she defined as a felt sense of energy, rhythm, or intuitive knowing that occurs in groups and which positively influences the way they interact toward a common purpose. For her doctoral research, she studied over thirty group situations in which this experience was reported, ranging from a construction site to a sailing expedition. Consistently she found the experience of vulnerability, in a group member or the group as a whole, to be the key shifting factor that allowed the group members to move into deeper resonance with each other. From this experience of vulnerability came a more profound level of healing, community, and creation.

Levi tells a particularly poignant story of a young single mother diagnosed with cancer and facing the uncertainty of her treatment. The woman decided to gather her close women friends together and create a healing community around herself. The story, as told by one of the women who participated in the group, revealed the intricate relationships of healing and ritual, and the power of friendship. Shortly after she was first diagnosed, "she organized a healing evening on the beach with her closest friends, those she felt would understand this concept. She felt strongly about the power of a group. . . . We blindfolded her, we carried her down to the beach. She did nothing, she just received. We sang songs to her, we put cream on her, we had smells that she could sort of relish in, we brushed her hair. . . .

"In addition to that healing group on the beach, we also went back to her house, brainstormed, figured out what she needed to do in terms of her work because she's a single mom. We helped her get together a schedule for her children to be watched while she was doing her therapy, and that part in itself was very magical. Here were these eight women bustling around. We had all our children with us. There was no arguing between the children. They would all go off and play together. . . . It set the tone, and there were several other situations where we gathered together like this."[3]

Here we have an exquisite example of intentionally creating a field of belonging, a place in which a group is in agreement to create an emotional field for healing and also preparing for the future work that will be necessary. Cooperation, meaning literally a method of operating together, entailed both the ritualistic element of a healing ceremony and the "bustling around," creating the new structures necessary for the woman's ongoing care. The group's actions are neither a cure nor mere to-do lists; the friends are coming together to do what is necessary and practical for the interior world and the material one. There is also a larger social element, for we learn that part of the woman's efforts were to address abusive elements of her own painful family ancestry. "I think this is a generation of women," reflected her friend, "who are really determined to end the unconscious cycles that are in their families, whether it's sexual abuse or alcoholism, or whatever those pieces are. And they're saying, 'I'm not going to pass this on.'"

By creating a sense of caring and authentic engagement, we are prototyping a more hopeful future, and we are also learning from and honoring the wounds that have been handed down to us from our past. The cross-cultural anthropologist Angeles Arrien put it best when she told us how she now views the focus on the group and collective: "I think that collective work, group work, organizational work, and community work can heal family dynamics or continue to repeat them. A time where we say 'Enough, already.' Or an experience where you're seen and heard and have made a contribution. I think the human spirit always wants to make a contribution. And I don't think there are enough invitations."[4]

CONFLICT AS AN INVITATION FOR A HIGHER ORDER OF RESOLUTION

Colonel Stas Preczewski faced an exasperating problem. He was the coach of the crew team at West Point and had chosen his most skilled rowers for the varsity team. His problem was that the junior varsity team was beating them consistently. Individually, he did not doubt that he had chosen the right rowers, but collectively, they appeared to be more competitive with each other than with their opposition. One day, he lined up his eight rowers into four pairs and told them that they would wrestle each other for ninety seconds. No punches, no intent to hurt the other, but they were to wrestle the other rower to the ground. Soon, they discovered just how strong and determined each one of them was. Preczewski had them change opponents and wrestle again, and by the third round, rowers were choosing each other. One of the rowers started laughing, and it became contagious, the group piling onto each other in a collective brawl. Finally, one of the teammates asked the coach if they could go row. From resentment and competition with each other, they moved toward appreciation and cooperation. The story is, from that day on, their boat flew.[5]

Although we might wish that all conflict resolution could be this easy or at least less physical, there is a critical lesson here. Tensions need to find a way to the surface and to be worked out in ways that cultivate respect and regard for each other and the group's task. We each need to see others as purposeful and contributing positively; when we don't, competition and conflict become wounding rather than a creative tension.

Healing is necessary for those in conflict precisely because wounding occurs on the inside, where we do not see it. And it is often what we don't see that sabotages external efforts to move forward and find common ground. In order for individuals and groups to "get beyond" past obstacles, there must be some redress for the emotional pain that has been experienced. Similarly, attempts to address feelings isolated from external changes do not have the gravitas to anchor new behaviors. We need everything from new insights to new agreements to move beyond conflicted group dynamics. Specifically, groups need the experience of devising, shaping, and discovering new possibilities among themselves. This is why simply imposing solutions from outside typically does not work. There is no creativity in passivity.

Conflict can be an invitation for a higher order of resolution. This means listening, deciphering, and unlocking new alternatives. It means achieving a new understanding of the situation and grasping the basic needs of all those involved. Conflict has the potential to draw us into new areas of introspection and reveal the hidden complexity of a situation. It often entails grappling with paradox and allowing all the different layers of history to come into a new alignment.

Reconciliation of these forces requires seeing ourselves as part of an expanded community. We begin to recognize diversity as part of that larger community and seek ways to lessen the historical toxicity that invariably keeps us stuck in old patterns. Tom Hurley, former managing director of the Chaordic Alliance and a writer on collective wisdom practices, describes one particular example of institutional reconciliation among fishermen, environmentalists, and business owners who came together to form the Northwest Atlantic Marine Alliance:

"These groups had spent years at war with one another. The fishermen and environmentalists, of course, had been in court a number of times, and in some cases the fishermen had literally been in shooting wars with one another, in disputes over fishing grounds and that sort of thing. In working with this group, we brought people to the table who had a history of ill will, mistrust and resentment toward one another. We knew they'd never agree to any concept for a new organization that came from only one subset of stakeholders. The environmentalists could never have drafted a purpose statement that the fishermen would have accepted, nor would one group of fishermen have been trusted, by the others, to understand or articulate the interests of all.

"What the work required was just sitting down with these individuals day after day and getting them to tell their stories, to talk about the truth of their experience—which not only included the truth of their day-to-day work at sea or on land, but the truth of their lives as husbands, as parents, as sons and daughters, as citizens, and as members of a community whose health and vitality was threatened as the marine ecosystem declined. Only in listening to the truth of the personal stories that individuals told, in beginning to feel the passion that all of them felt for their lives and the sea—whose well-being they cared deeply about—did they begin to get through the barriers . . . getting beyond putting one another into a category."[6]

The "work" in this example is the awareness that healing involves greater transparency of the whole person and system. Time was spent reflecting on day-to-day issues, as well as on the individuals' roles as family members, citizens, and members of a community who shared a love for their lives on the sea. The ability to listen to their own interior voices and then make it safe enough to listen to the interior voices of others brought out a whole new quality of interaction, one closer to inquiry and empathy than debate. It's within such a field of engagement that we begin to pay attention to each other as human, with all the complexity, contradictions, and paradoxes that implies. As the categories that people typically put each other into softened, a more encompassing order began to emerge.

"We never," Hurley told us, "could have talked with that group about 'emotional intelligence'—but as they honestly expressed emotion, from anger and distrust to empathy and exhilaration, they developed a trust in themselves and one another that eventually supported a capacity for working constructively in the service of what they cared most deeply about, in ways that they couldn't have previously imagined." The shift represented a more hopeful perspective toward the future, a reframing of their circumstances rather than a simple compromise among competing factions.

Collective wisdom often entails a shift away from strategies based on winning and dominance and toward constructive engagement and learning. What emerges is conscious intention to seek out what might work for all, even when that path seems blocked or strewn with obstacles. Groups become more inclined to operate from a commitment to acknowledging their differences and respecting each other in the process. They are more willing to suspend certainty in order to seek common ground and become more fluent in allowing into conversation the interior experience of their members.

As collective wisdom emerges, group members begin to comprehend how much of the conflict is structural, built into the ways things have previously been designed. There is a re-assessment of power in particular. A group begins to grasp that the situation will not change unless *we change*. From this orientation, groups can begin to make better sense of their opportunities and the obstacles they face. Hurley noted that even during the time when the alliance was still struggling to form beneficial community agreements, the group served as a creative context for conflict resolution and problem solving in the members' separate communities. They had made a shift toward treating each other as equals, sharing power, and accepting the bumps in the road. They had become healthy cells in a larger social body.

CULTIVATING OUR MORAL IMAGINATION

In 1999, CIDA (Community and Individual Development Association) City Campus opened its doors in Johannesburg, South Africa, to the "poorest of the poor" so that they might earn a four-year degree in business. Six months prior, Barbara

Nussbaum,[7] one of our colleagues, and Taddy Blecher, a cofounder of the enterprise, traveled through the streets of the city looking for a building that might be suitable. They shared a dream of education rooted in the very real challenges of post-apartheid South Africa. There must have been times when they wondered what they were doing.

IN A COUNTRY BURDENED BY poverty and crime, Johannesburg is one of its most dangerous cities. In 1998, a year before CIDA opened, South Africa had the highest recorded per capita murder rate of countries selected for study by Interpol: fifty-nine recorded murders per hundred thousand of the population, followed by Colombia with fifty-six. In contrast, Spain had three murders per hundred thousand and Canada had four.

During its first year of operation, CIDA had no computers, a problem for business students and especially those who had no access to a computer of their own. Most of the students did not even know how to type. Undaunted, Blecher made 250 photocopies of a computer keyboard and monitor for the students. "Students learned skills on imaginary computers," Nussbaum recalled, "by typing rhythmically to songs like Bob Marley's 'Redemption Song'—'Emancipate yourselves from mental slavery; none but ourselves can free our minds.'" Several months later, when companies eventually started donating older computers (mostly 326s), most of the students had mastered a typing speed above thirty words a minute.

The story is an illustration of how healing and imagination can be joined with creative work and community. The founders of CIDA perceived the link between one small part, in this case creating imaginary computers, and the larger goal of demonstrating a belief that nothing is impossible if we alter our mental outlook. Today, CIDA has become an internationally recognized success, with four campuses; hundreds of graduates; and new programs, like the CIDA School of Investments, sponsored through business partnerships with J.P. Morgan, Reuters, and the Johannesburg Stock Exchange.

The desires to repair our social world and heal social chaos are twin forces latent in even the direst circumstances. Yet the desire to actually change requires individuals, partnerships, teams, and networks to act on what's possible. We might say that all group fields have this potential—to cultivate one, then two, then many who can bring these possibilities forward. Nussbaum told us that Blecher had always been inspired by the proverb, "Weave and the thread will follow." Collective wisdom—a depth of awareness, insight, and transcendent knowing leading to profound action—often begins from a small intuitive seed and grows with imagination. Group members come to trust that if we tend to what is most immediate and aligned with purpose, the thread of a larger pattern will reveal itself.

The psychiatrist Stanislav Grof coined the term *holotropic* to suggest an extraordinary human capacity in the brain to move from part to whole. He believes that in our body and mind lies an extraordinary healing capacity to reconstruct, from the smallest positive images, a larger healthier whole.

Grof has used this principle in aiding cancer patients, but its implications are also organizational. Healing and imagination work together to excite the parts of our mind generating holograms of a life-affirming whole. Our minds can sense in any genuine action of caring and empathy a larger possibility for the collective. Our work becomes less about changing people than about designing environments that arouse the healing and creative impulses latent in each of us and in groups.

There is one further lesson in CIDA's use of imaginary computers. Often, in the difficult circumstances of our lives and organizations, we are reluctant to allow our imaginations to roam too far or to pursue these more life-affirming "big pictures." We are understandably cowed by the extent of need or intimidated by reminders from others that we live in the "real world" and not the world of our imagination. We fear that our imagination is simply a form of pretending, meaning an illusion.

The story of creating imaginary computers to assist students who are without resources has metaphoric power: We see that in order to tend to problems of the world, we sometimes have to pre-tend, meaning to make full use of our imagination and create a prototype of a future that is felt to be right and just. "If I don't tend to it before I get there," Rabbi Zalman Schachter-Shalomi told us mischievously, explaining how he uses the word *pretend*, "then I'll never get there."[8] Before we can effectively address social healing, we need to do the interior work of a moral imagination, what some may discount as illusion because they cannot see the greater wisdom that lies beneath the surface.

The work of collective wisdom invites our whole selves—the interior work of our imagination and the external acts of invention. We can and must emancipate ourselves, rang out the song that played in the background of the students' typing, from mental slavery. Together, we can free our minds.

SEEING THE FUTURE IN THE PRESENT MOMENT: HIDDEN IN PLAIN VIEW

> *Love alone is capable of uniting living beings in such a way as to complete and fulfill them, for it alone takes them and joins them by what is deepest in themselves. . . . Does not love every instant achieve all around us, in the couple or the team, the magic feat . . . of "personalising" by totalising? And if that is what it can achieve daily on a small scale, why should it not repeat this one day on world-wide dimensions?*
>
> —Pierre Teilhard de Chardin, *The Phenomenon of Man*

The Center for Empowering Refugees and Immigrants (CERI), in Oakland, California, is a powerful example of community, mediated by love. The fact that it evolved as a response to the wounds generated by war, torture, and genocide makes it a telling illustration of what power lies in the group. Empowerment came from amplifying existing elements of group cohesion, respect for interior realms, and desire to repair and renew the community.

Mona Afary,[9] who helped found the center, tells this story as testament to the Cambodian community that she has come to know:

"PERSEPHONE, IN GREEK MYTHOLOGY, WAS fourteen when she was abducted and taken to the underworld. The underworld was dark and gloomy; it was the realm of the ghosts, dead and lost souls who had no connection to what had happened to them. Like Persephone, they were abruptly stripped of what they knew as life and brought to darkness, confused as to why this tragedy had come to be. With the support of her powerful mother, Demeter, the goddess of Earth, and Hermes, the god of communication, Persephone was eventually able to leave the underworld for three seasons a year, but was doomed to go back every winter. In spring when she would return to earth, all would blossom and flourish . . . upon her return to the underworld in winter, the whole earth would mourn and perish.

"Year after year, Persephone lived in utter depression in the underworld. At one point, she eventually regained the strength to communicate with the dead who were twisted in their tragic losses. One by one, they began sharing their stories and for the first time were honored for them. The silence and confusion and fear began to gradually dissipate.

"The Cambodian refugees at CERI have somewhat of a similar experience as this myth. The majority of them were living a peaceful life as children, teens, or young adults in the rural parts of Cambodia. The brutal regime of Pol Pot, also known as the Khmer Rouge, took over between the years 1975 and 1978, and before they knew it, their beloved country was transformed into their own concentration camp, in which they were forced to work twelve to sixteen hours with only one meal a day, consisting of a cup of water with a few grains of rice.

"One million seven hundred thousand Cambodians died, many from exhaustion, illness, and starvation. Every evening, when the sun would set, the Khmer Rouge would enter these people's homes, taking families to an area which is now referred to as the Killing Fields, beating them to death.

"Our clients are the survivors of this atrocious genocide. Forced to flee their homeland, they sought safety in dangerous Thai refugee camps. Years later, when they were finally able to settle in Oakland, they were placed in poor and high-crime neighborhoods."

When Mona Afary was first hired as a mental health counselor, she faced the clients' stories alone, seeing and feeling their acute pain in the form of their nightmares, insomnia, flashbacks, panic attacks, depression, anxiety, fear, unmourned grief, and physical disorders that accompany such psychological pain. What hope could they have of a future?

And then something startling happened one day. Afary came out of her counseling office and encountered, in the waiting room, a Cambodian community drinking American coffee and Persian tea. They were talking and laughing and knitting together. What, she wondered, would happen if the possibility for healing were already present, sitting here amid the group, in the waiting room? This was the small spark that gave rise to CERI, but not immediately. First, there needed to be validation that this idea could attract others, this notion that the group itself could truly be a source of its own empowerment. How could the same informality of gathering and sense of affection for each other that Afary witnessed in the waiting room be retained and extended?

Collective wisdom holds the possibility of creating new organizational forms that are inclusive, invitational, and sacred without being overly earnest. This is how CERI emerged. In short order, Afary developed a partnership with a Cambodian woman, Lucy Dul, who had arrived as a child refugee herself and had started a nonprofit agency to address the social needs of her community. Soon, a group interpreter was found, a genocide survivor, and many other gifted part-time people followed, contributing their talents, including offering counseling encounters in the streets with Cambodian children who were cutting classes during the day. An experienced homeopathic clinician began volunteering her time, and soon two other practitioners were also contributing their talents. When the emerging group lost the services of their psychiatrist, a board member of the community agency that Afary had worked for volunteered to substitute and soon "fell in love" and committed himself to offering pro bono support. Afary's clinical supervisor and her former dissertation chair also joined the growing movement, as did the Cambodian monks who were already part of the community.

A nurturing field of relationships was born, animated by activities of belonging that showed that life had come into the group. A sewing machine, knitting, painting, chanting, prayer, yoga, meditation, movement, and massage therapy all appeared as part of a community forming itself into a whole. A year after Afary's experience in the waiting room, the organization was formally born. It was hard work but also play.

Collective wisdom can be an act of transcendence, a testament that we are not as separate as we think. Psychologist Daniel Goleman, addressing the role of mirror neurons in the brain, reminds us that humans are capable of not only mimicking the actions of others but reading intentions and emotions that allow for "a shared sensibility, bringing the outside inside us: to understand another, we become like the other—at least a bit."[10]

The implications of this are essential for the emergence of collective wisdom in groups because it tells us that we can know what others are feeling and intending. Quoting the developmental scientist Daniel Stern, Goleman goes on to say we can "no longer 'see our minds as so independent, separate and isolated,' but instead we must view them as 'permeable,' continually interacting as though joined by an invisible link. At an unconscious level, we are in constant dialogue with anyone we interact with, our every feeling and our every way of moving attuned to theirs. At least for the moment our mental life is cocreated, in an interconnected two-person matrix."[11]

Mona Afary is one of those individuals who did not see herself as separate. She knew that healing comes from the impulse for creation, for reaching out and extending ourselves to others. "Now here is where our story deviates from the myth of Persephone and the underworld," she told us. "Our Cambodian friends have changed. They know that they are the pillars of strength and inspiration for one another. They have gained the strength to be with their losses without allowing the pain to ruin their lives any further. This community has started a new chapter in its life. They are the cofounders of CERI, and they want to use it as a means to leave the underworld as a community."

SUMMARY: COLLECTIVE WISDOM EMERGING

What is striking about all these stories is just how full of life, surprising, and down to earth they are. Individuals, productive partnerships, small groups, and committed communities are seedbeds for new collective visions weaving themselves together. Whether forming a literary club or a personal healing community, we all need to cultivate hope with those who nourish us, challenge us, and seek to know our talents and gifts. If we are dealing with conflict, we need to respect others as equals, with determination similar to our own. We need to believe that it is possible to find a higher order of resolution, shifting from solely a position of debate to one of inquiry. Should we turn to the reality of social dislocation and social inequalities, we might remember Taddy Blecher and Barbara Nussbaum driving through the streets of Johannesburg—it's useful to partner with someone and seek a physical base for dreams that are inspired in our imagination. And like Mona Afary, we might draw faith that our answers are right in front of us, if we have the courage and the "worldview" to see our community differently.

Collective wisdom emerges over time in relationship to immediate needs and larger visions. It is a way of working with others that integrates what is practical, tangible, and resilient with the twists and turns that constitute the road of life. Collective wisdom invariably involves possibilities, opportunities barely glimpsed and some yet to be imagined. Neither solely about a moment of profound insight nor isolated to one person or group, collective wisdom is a deepening of collective understanding; it is the way we can come together to address our social world and the need for its repair.

By now, the critical elements of collective wisdom woven throughout this chapter can be pointed out. The stance of seeing whole systems suggests that we honor different perspectives as fundamental to the whole. Group discernment reflects the range of needs—material, emotional, and spiritual—that we have as human beings. Deep listening is an invitation to others to bring out their true selves. The stances of collective wisdom teach us that the bonds we create with others matter and are critical for sustainable group efforts. In these stories, we observe also the trust in the transcendent element of human endeavor, courage in the face of uncertainty, and humility in light of seemingly overwhelming odds that we do not control.

Finally, woven into these stories is a regard for emergence itself as a fundamental human impulse. Emergence brings into existence something original. When groups are involved with the emergent aspects of collective discovery, it is always the first time. Emergence is about new forms, new perspectives, and new ways to think about or see a situation. The personal element of emergence is emotional and subjective, meaning that we feel it inside ourselves, suffused with our deepest values. There is an inner knowing and sense of excitement—what is unfolding, what is being revealed? Creation as a function of emergence, alongside healing, community, and moral imagination, becomes an extension of our human capacity for joy. We know ourselves as part of something larger, not as something separate or alone. Emergence in groups is the experience of bringing into manifestation something elusive but worthwhile. Whether alone or in a group, the creativity associated with emergence always has the energy of making, devising, producing, shaping. When aligned with addressing the needs we see in the world, creation of this type is a form of love. And it is always collective, whether it comes through an individual or the group.

eight

Practices of Mindfulness for Collective Wisdom

All of the stories in this book and the research behind them suggest that there is common ground beyond what commonly separates us. We draw from this one conclusion: There is still more to be discovered in our fellowship with others that can lead to the freedom and creative potential of human communities.

In this concluding chapter, we address four mindfulness practices that allow us to maintain commitments and convictions that foster collective wisdom's emergence. Our assumption is that without a personal practice of continuous and vigilant mindfulness, no set of behaviors, plans, checklists, or models can be reliable. Mindfulness practices are simply ways of paying attention to our own inner experience and outer engagement with the world. They help us to focus the mind and re-mind ourselves of our true intent.

At its most basic, *mindfulness* is defined as a mental state characterized by concentrated awareness of one's thoughts, actions, and motivations. Mindfulness plays a central role in Eastern teachings and increasingly is being incorporated into Western practices for good reason. It is a long-held tradition identified with engendering insight and wisdom.

Mindfulness is a gentle practice for deepening reflection because it continually returns us to the present moment. By noticing, for example, the continual commentary within our own mind, we can observe more closely the nature of our thought without judgment. We begin to become aware that "thoughts are just thoughts," not edicts that should rule our behavior. By practicing being alert to the present moment, we begin to recognize what is happening in us and around us. If what is happening is worry, concern, or despair, we need to act immediately. Similarly, if we are in groups and become aware of anxiety, fear, or conflict, this too alerts us to the need for finding new perspectives and taking actions that re-frame and redirect our energies.

For our purposes, mindfulness practice can be a tool for further enabling collective wisdom to arise. By bringing our attention back to the present moment, we continually re-mind ourselves to be present to others and purposeful in our actions. The four mindfulness practices we describe here can be practiced individually, but they are meant to serve the collective awakening of groups:

1   • First is the practice of creating safe spaces for inquiry, an essential element for enabling groups to have the reflective time necessary to birth new insights and make sound judgments.

2   • Second is a practice that enables deep listening, the stance we have discussed throughout this book.

3   • The third practice involves shifting our attention from seeing individual experts to recognizing the power of group expertise.

4   • Finally is the practice of learning to ask essential questions, which teaches us that we can impact external circumstances by the questions we choose to focus on.

MINDFULNESS PRACTICE:
CREATING SAFE SPACES FOR INQUIRY

We saw in Tom Hurley's description of the Northwest Atlantic Marine Alliance the creation of space for awakening curiosity in the "other" and allowing new agreements to become possible. We saw, particularly in the ways that polarization and false agreements have led to tragedy, the dangers of collapsing the space for inquiry. In the last decade, we have witnessed an explosion of group methodologies and processes that seek to make visible the "wisdom" that is among us and coming through us. These methodologies include various forms of dialogue; organizational interventions such as Appreciative Inquiry and stakeholder engagement; and avenues through which groups can catalyze new insights, such as those developed by our colleagues Juanita Brown and David Isaacs in the format of the World Café.

Fundamental to all these group methodologies is a response to the need to be understood. Anyone who has worked with children knows how deeply rooted this human impulse is. It goes beyond individual temperament or mood. Being understood is akin to experiencing love, and being mindful of this need for understanding brings our attention automatically to how we impact others. Actions as simple as spending an extra moment greeting others and showing our regard for them create the conditions in which they can feel safe and more open to exploration.

Ultimately, however, it is the value system behind the actions that matters. A physician colleague notes that patients don't care how much you know; they want to know how much you care. In the medical office, caring is what creates safety. His comment captures the spirit behind the practice of making spaces safe for inquiry. When people are in groups, we first want to know we are safe, and our feeling of being safe or unsafe precedes a willingness to engage honestly with others.

Beyond basic safety, we want to be with others in ways that recognize who we are, that celebrate our talents, and that allow us to contribute. Creating safe spaces for inquiry makes us mindful that it is important for individuals to feel both unique and part of the group. When this basic need is frustrated, we stop being interested in what the group or collective can do. Sadly, the effect on how the group operates is similar to how the brain operates in instances of autism: Pockets of expertise, even genius, remain, but there is no larger orchestration of the multiple forms of intelligence—

physical, cognitive, spiritual, and emotional—that constitute the group as a whole.

When we create safe spaces for inquiry, we are inviting in our whole selves: what we really feel and sense inside ourselves, what truly matters to us, and what we can discover together with others. We are mindful that what creates safety for inquiry are the possibilities of being understood and keeping our dignity intact. We create safety by designing settings where there is opportunity for reflection and curiosity, often as a counterpoint to meetings where deadlines and immediate survival are at stake. In the NASA story, the tragedy was not only in the final moments of forced agreement, but in the whole chain of events that allowed a critical variable to go unresolved.

Creating safe space for inquiry can be counterintuitive. When conflict emerges, our reaction is often to contract and become more isolated. A mindfulness practice can be to notice an inclination in ourselves to become rigid and dogmatic. Instead of acting from a habitual stance of wanting to be right, we can gently redirect our attention to examining our assumptions and inquiring into what is possible with others.

Safety for inquiry is created by listening with respect, even to those with whom we may differ. We can practice this, and notice when this capability within ourselves becomes strained or if our attention wanders. Through this practice, we can become aware that change is not only for the other, but also about how *we* will need to change as well.

Change is often accompanied by a power shift between individuals or groups. As we move deeper into this practice, we will notice that as difficult as it may be to establish respectful relations with an adversarial foe, it is equally challenging to become "licensed" by one's own group to pursue a positive relationship with an "other." We must be prepared to address the resistance that is natural in groups when familiar patterns are threatened.

An underlying assumption of this mindfulness practice is that we see that things must be fundamentally different, not just incrementally better. It is the vision that Mary Parker Follett described almost a century ago. We recognize that the future is created with others, even those with whom we differ. Paradox is embraced because we begin to see that stopping conflict cannot be a precondition for creating the safe space for dialogue. We need to establish safety amid uncertainty. We do this in part by shifting our attention from difficult personalities to structural impediments and the places where common ground can be found. Together, we can search for opportunities not previously seen.

PRACTICES FOR CREATING SAFE SPACES FOR INQUIRY

Guiding Intent: Recognizing the need for people to be understood.

> *First Self-Observation:* Notice how caring for others in groups makes it possible to deepen exploration and inquiry.

> *Personal Practice:* Direct your attention to what makes others distinctive and positive contributors to the group. Look for opportunities to voice these observations out loud in the group or directly to the individual.

Second Self-Observation: Notice times when you are inclined to become rigid, judgmental, or dogmatic.

Personal Practice: Direct your attention to examining your own expectations and assumptions or to how you feel misunderstood or marginalized. Look for opportunities to articulate differences without polarizing or forcing your opinions on others.

MINDFULNESS PRACTICE: DEEP LISTENING

Deep listening is a form of mindfulness that continually returns our attention to a deeper ground of being. Paula Underwood introduced us to a useful tenet of deep listening. It is that the intimacy of listening to one person is coherent with listening to the universe. As you may recall from chapter 2, when Underwood's father asked her if she could hear his friend's "heart," her instinct was to place her ear to the chests of the people she knew. She was learning how to pay attention literally to the beats and rhythms of the heart. As she grew into the role of clan mother, deep listening was a way of listening to others on behalf of the needs, desires, and dreams of a larger community.

To know the people's hearts, she had to learn how to listen "between the lines" and even when people were not speaking. "If you want to truly listen to someone else," she told us, "you must empty yourself and let them fill the emptiness. There must be nothing inside you but a great willingness to hear, to listen. . . . It's as if you are nearly starving and someone is offering you food. When you can listen like that, then you can truly hear."[1]

Deep listening is a practice of emptying out the noise and rattle that accompanies much of our own thoughts. It is finding a quiet space in our own mind that allows us to "sense" into the other. Underwood compares it to physical hunger, where we become so receptive to the words and associated meanings of others that it feels like a satisfying meal. The psychologist and science journalist Daniel Goleman has a distinct but related way of describing this, as discussed in chapter 7. Mirror neurons have been identified within the architecture of the physical brain that allow us—at least a bit—to sense the intentions and emotions of others. Deep listening is a practice of deepening this natural empathic connection that we have in common with others—seeing, if just for an instant, through the eyes of others.

Deep listening as a mindfulness practice extends listening and sensing to groups and larger collectives. This requires us to first quiet the many voices in our own mind. *Monkey mind* is the Buddhist term for how our internal thoughts jump from thing to thing in the same way that a monkey jumps from tree to tree. Monkey mind does not allow us to be receptive to others because it is never content with the present moment, always shifting back and forth between past and future.

Deep listening, by contrast, is always in the present moment, allowing thoughts to bind together. Each thought occupies its own space and extends into the next one. In this way, the perspectives of others gain enough space to take on their own significance, yet they remain connected to the larger group field. The more we practice a mindfulness that encompasses the whole, the greater the chance that an under-lying order can be perceived.

Deep listening, as Underwood suggested, can be translated into a different kind of presence in groups. Ben Zander, con-ductor of the Boston Philharmonic, once told Nelson Mandela that he was the "the first leader of Symphonia." "What is that?" asked Mandela, with a raised eyebrow. Zander explained that the word *symphony* is a combination of *sym* ("together") and *phonae* ("to sound")—the sounding together of all the voices. "You are," Zander said, "the first leader of Symphonia, because instead of leading in the traditional way from the top down, you focused on allowing all the voices to be heard." Mandela thought for a moment and smiled. "I like that."[2]

As a practice, deep listening can be experienced as a gen-tle detachment from the commentary in our own mind and a turning to others. In groups, we can do this in the imme-diacy of the moment by simple acts such as observing the expression on another's face or even the clothes someone is wearing. We deepen the practice by acting with a purpose-ful intent to listen to the whole person, which is different from simply hearing the other person speak. Deep listening is a practice that allows us to read between the lines and listen with our heart to the hearts of others.

PRACTICES FOR DEEP LISTENING

Guiding Intent: To cultivate empathy and understanding in groups. Listening with intent to understand more than what is actually being said.

First Self-Observation: Notice your own state of mind. Empathy requires a measure of personal calmness to listen well to others.

Personal Practice: Direct your attention to what aids calmness. For some, it is attention to breath, taking a moment to breathe deeply and relax the body. For others, it may involve sitting quietly for a few extra moments. Still others take time for a personal inventory, noticing feelings and thoughts arising that signal fear or agitation, or, alternatively, calmness and appreciation. Practice noticing your thoughts and gently inhabiting a more open and calm presence with others.

Second Self-Observation: Notice how you feel resonance and connection with others. How does your body respond when you are feeling connected with others? Do you lean forward, physically relax, feel warmth spreading from your heart to the rest of your body? How do your head and heart operate together when you are listening deeply to another? Do you become aware of greater focus and concentration? Do you become more aware of symbol and metaphor? Can you sense what is "between the lines" of what you are hearing?

Personal Practice: Direct your attention outward, practicing being nourished by the unique ways people have of expressing themselves. Notice and give voice to what you find surprising, delightful, and unique in what others are saying.

MINDFULNESS PRACTICE:
MOVING FROM INDIVIDUAL EXPERTS TO
GROUP EXPERTISE

When we consider the power of collective wisdom as a whole, we begin to see a profound—even evolutionary—transition under way: We are moving from a culture of individualism and individual experts to collective forms of knowing and the expertise of teams and groups. Foreshadowed in the historical documents of democracy, advanced by pioneers such as Mary Parker Follett and Pierre Teilhard de Chardin, lived out in indigenous traditions, and reanimated by social pioneers today, this change is appearing as the branching movement of human evolution. Collective awakening is the moment when groups, communities, nations, and by extension global networks begin to wake up to the interconnectedness of our lives on this planet.

An individual's finding a community of like-minded people is a first step, but we cannot stop there. This is a critical time in human history for our visions of a better world to be represented in tangible forms. Finding such forms requires tolerance for uncertainty and faith that what is still unknown will reveal itself in positive growth. It is a commitment to constructive engagement that does not come with preconditions. The mindfulness of such a stance invites us to continually learn from our actual circumstances and not be limited by dogmatic ideas or conventional wisdom. Our guide will be our own reflection on experience and an inner intent for finding ways to cooperate with others. Seeking to free our minds of fear, we might recall Einstein's words that we have the power to correct for the "optical delusion" of our separateness.

The movement from individual experts to group expertise is a way of recognizing that "we" can be more effective than any one "I" in the room. This is not because groups always make sound judgments—our book raises severe cautions about how foolishness and its tragic consequences arise in groups—but because getting things done requires many people synchronized together. Similarly, there are many examples of one individual getting it right when the larger group gets it wrong. This is our point—if the group cannot recognize the wisdom within its own sphere, contained even in the dissenting member, it will be vulnerable as a whole group. We saw this lesson in the stories of unsanitary practices at Vienna General Hospital and of NASA's inability to listen to warnings of its spaceships' potential defects, as well as in countless examples since, from the Iraq invasion to global warming to the collapse of major financial institutions.

Collective wisdom requires groups to constantly experiment with ways of synthesizing diverse information, listening for dissent, and understanding what is beneath the passions of the moment. Leadership is needed to nourish the mind and spirit in order for agreements and directed action to be expressions of the group itself—not edicts from above or expert-driven solutions that do not relate to the actual circumstances of the situation. This is what Paula Underwood addressed in her understanding of *one mind* and Jerry Sternin discovered for himself in the rural lands of Vietnam, a discovery that gave birth to his elaboration of the concept of positive deviance.

The shift from individual experts to group expertise requires continual awareness of our tendency to fall back on habitual behaviors, particularly a false reliance on hierarchy for solutions and unconscious habits of dominance over others. Seeking collective wisdom in groups is an invitation for transparency of operations, involving such things as real-time data, group huddles, and opportunities for both individual and team reflection.

In groups, the benefit of mindfulness is that greater attention is paid to what is *actually* happening. The immediate effect is the opportunity for mitigating errors that arise spontaneously and redirecting energies toward new behaviors and positive outcomes. We keep in mind that people in positions of hierarchical authority are always coming and going. Manuals and policies are forever changing. What is most useful is the cultivation of a group's know-how to achieve excellence. This means empowering people closest to the work and keeping all members of the group conscious of their alignment with higher purpose.

Shifting our reliance from individual experts to group expertise builds resilience. Groups need to continue functioning despite setbacks. No improvements can be sustained if a group is dependent on everything going right from the beginning or on any one individual. A group's ability to develop resilience allows it to feel safe enough to see what is *not* going right and to improvise as needed. This builds confidence that failures do not need to become permanent and that successes are not dependent on factors outside the group's control. We might be reminded of the spontaneous behavior that Lauren Artress described on the labyrinth in response to the stranger who crumpled to the floor weeping. We are not immune to unforeseen developments that may appear as obstacles, but groups have the capacity to overcome them and contribute to a better outcome.

PRACTICES FOR MOVING FROM INDIVIDUAL EXPERTS TO GROUP EXPERTISE

Guiding Intent: To learn how to pay attention to connectedness and interdependence in groups and larger collectives.

First Self-Observation: Notice how you pay attention to the collective. Are you aware primarily of individual efforts, or of relationships, partnerships, and teams that work together on behalf of common goals?

Personal Practice: Direct your attention to what aids success in groups. For some, this may mean reminding people of what has already been accomplished; for others it may mean focusing attention on an underlying purpose that joins people together. Practice noticing how groups achieve a better understanding of their situation or build a collective will to accomplish their goals. Remember that every group is unique, so the avenues for development will be particular to each group and each situation.

Second Self-Observation: Notice your own answers to the question, what expertise is necessary for groups to be successful? In a group setting, pay attention to who

contributes technical expertise, who holds the group together during times of stress, who maintains the vision,
who provides structure. How is interdependence necessary to achieve the best results?

Personal Practice: Direct your energy to learning what is
required for a successful outcome. From a stance of curiosity, discuss with as many people as possible what they
do and how it is connected to a larger outcome.

MINDFULNESS PRACTICE: ASKING ESSENTIAL QUESTIONS

The most practical form of mindfulness is embodied in the
questions that focus our attention on what matters most.
Questions stimulate the imagination, which is our most profound defense against habitual thinking and normative pressures. The following five questions are starting points for
continually renewing the here-and-now experience of group
life and drawing us back to beginner's mind.

What is alive here and now? This is a question for practicing
seeing into one's own mind and, by extension, seeing into the
collective mind of the group. How am I feeling? What feels
alive in my own body, or conversely, what feels numb or dis-
connected? In analogous fashion, notice the environment in
which you come together in groups—the physical setting and
arrangement of space, emotional tone, and initial encounters
of group members. Do people seem excited, invigorated, un-
certain, reflective, distracted, anticipatory? Are people asked

to share some of their thoughts and feelings? Do they feel that their experience and knowledge are seen and welcomed? What interactions shift the tone or energy of a room? These are the kinds of observations about oneself and others that relate to what is happening in the moment, and they are part of the recognition that groups are continually changing, transforming, and remaking themselves.

What is the context for encounter? Looking at context in its simplest form is having an alert awareness to three-dimensional space and paying attention to our physical and emotional environments. How we face each other in a circle or across a long boardroom table matters. How we allow the outside world in or stay shut up in windowless rooms matters. Noticing context is an interactive process involving relationships of people and natural elements.

In a broader sense, looking at context involves awareness of a group's or organization's culture. It draws our attention to the unique circumstances of the group and how power is negotiated. Differences in power may be attributed to institutional hierarchy, seniority, prior experience, or professional certification, but regardless of the reasons, groups can better access a way of knowing collectively by softening the edges of power differentials. We honor the wisdom emerging among us when we acknowledge each other's contribution, rather than confirming each other's relative position in the group.

One of the key observations made about the decisions that led to the *Challenger* tragedy was the differential of power in the group. The engineers were marginalized by the senior administrators just at the moment when the fateful judgment had to be made. Although we cannot dictate utopian solutions or simply ignore the fact that power differentials exist, we can bring attention to where expertise exists and shift from traditional ways of having *power over* others to ways of having *power with* them.

What is already working? This is a question that inspires hope and possibilities in groups, and of all the questions, it is the one that can most often be voiced out loud. The question is the basis for appreciative forms of inquiry where we seek what is already functional and positive. It is the counterintuitive response to focusing on what is missing and broken by expanding and encompassing more of what is working and valued.

The question of wanting to know what is already working was clearly demonstrated in our story about positive deviance, when Jerry Sternin gathered together data on children's growth by age and weight and asked who among the village had healthy, nourished children. The answer inspired an immediate visit to these families and the beginning of a strategy that worked for that village and eventually many others. The question is not about finding external best practices, but about learning how to replicate positive outcomes in each particular circumstance. We are seeking to know what is working now that can be built on. (For a greater discussion of this question, see *The Power of Appreciative Inquiry*, by Diana Whitney and Amanda Trosten-Bloom.[3])

What is being kept to the side? This is the question that allows us to be vigilant about the emergence of foolishness in groups. We discussed how folly often arises from unexamined assumptions that take on the qualities of truth, and how divergence is often directed into polarities or hidden under the veil of a false unity. The greatest obstacle to collective wisdom emerging is when one person or subgroup speaks on behalf of the whole and cannot be challenged. Sometimes the best collective decisions come forward only after an airing of differences and a recognition that those differences are still unresolved. Yet, we can still find what common ground exists in the moment. Jacob Needleman's story of Benjamin Franklin and the composing of the United States Constitution makes that abundantly clear.

When we ask ourselves what is being kept to the side, we are opening an inner eye to that which may not want to be seen. It is sometimes painful and disorienting. Yet practicing this question opens us up to new insights about how the group operates. We begin to see that we are different from each other and how clever the group can be in keeping some of those differences contained, marginalized, or explicitly shut down.

The question reminds us that we need to be constantly mindful of what is not said or shared. Our construct of community, for example, can include unstated elements of exclusion; shared intention may not be valued by individual group members; and our history of bias involving class, color, and notions of intelligence may be ignored to our collective detriment. Asking questions about what is not being discussed can feel like opening Pandora's box, but it can also be liberating when done in a way that is respectful of people and situations rather than as a means for feeling superior to others.

What is wanting to happen? This question allows us to peek around the corner of group process. By being still and observing all that is arising, we can see patterns of collective behavior and group aspirations. It is not a neutral activity, however, like some social scientist merely observing for purposes of study. We hold in our mind an intention for relationships that foster growth and the possibility of fairness, equity, and insight. Our eyes, ears, and physical body are now attuned to the collective and an image of what may be emergent, waiting to be born under the right circumstances. Margaret Mead noted, "Our humanity rests upon a series of learned behaviors, woven together into patterns that are infinitely fragile and never directly inherited." Through this question of what is wanting to happen, we are learning how to enter into the very weaving of our collective future. We are learning how to be a constructive part of cocreation. (For a greater discussion of this question, see *Theory U*, by C. Otto Scharmer.[4])

PRACTICES FOR ASKING ESSENTIAL QUESTIONS

Guiding Intent: To focus attention on the here-and-now experience of groups. To learn how we impact the development of groups by how and where we focus our attention.

> *First Self-Observation:* In group situations, notice how you pay attention to the immediacy of the moment. Are you aware of the physical environment and the people you

are with? Are you alert to how people look physically, the nature of their interactions, and the tone of the gathering? Are you open to what is arising in the moment, even if it is at times disturbing?

Personal Practice: Direct your attention to a group's ability to deal with the reality of its immediate situation. Practice gently bringing the group's attention to what is most likely on people's minds or weighs on them emotionally. For example, one of our colleagues told us a story of a meeting where a man had a heart attack and was taken away by ambulance. After he was gone, the meeting continued without any mention of what had just happened. Group members simply did not know the appropriate response to such a disturbing and fearful experience. Be alert that we do not all see the need to confront our immediate situation, and some of us find solace in denial. Consider yourself always a beginner, with a beginner's sensitivity, in helping to bring attention to what may be outside the group's awareness or is felt to be foreign or disturbing.

Second Self-Observation: Notice your personal response to the question of what is already working in the group. Often, we don't feel we are being "real" unless we are pointing to a problem or being critical of what has still not been accomplished.

Personal Practice: Direct your attention to what is already working in the group and practice talking about it openly with others. From a stance of appreciation, it is easier to face new challenges with past successes in mind. Keep in mind Jerry Sternin's advice that much of the conventional wisdom about why things don't work is TBU (true but useless). Practice discovering what does work and learn to ask why.

Have you ever noticed, after visiting an art museum or staring for a period of time at an extraordinary painting or photograph, that your way of seeing has been altered? Even mundane objects seem capable of beauty; subtleties of light and shadow become more pronounced, and our appreciation for the amazing world we live in becomes more tangible. Collective wisdom alters our way of seeing the world. If this book, even for brief moments, has guided you to dwell on the possibilities of what we can create together in groups, organizations, and larger collectives, then our efforts have been realized in your vision.

New ideas are often viewed as heretical, and few things are more subversive than the possibility that we can learn to respect each other, find ways to work out our differences, and deepen our capacity for wisdom. Cynics and pragmatists have every reason to question the limits of our human capacity to cooperate and contribute to a better world through collective action. Change of this kind and on this scale is unprecedented, and the history of human folly is well documented.

We do not need to argue, however, about change in the abstract. Collective change of this kind begins in small ways and spreads virally from one group to another, from one organization to another, from one network of visionaries and innovators into the larger public. Already, tremendous activity is permeating and percolating up through groups, networks, and communities. The diffusion of innovative ideas starts with a small group of people who have the ability to grasp new perspectives and apply them to the circumstances of their own situations. Collective wisdom as a field of study and practice is at the beginning of a very long learning curve—but one that already has tremendous vitality and moral imagination. Our hope is that this book has contributed a foundation for this emerging field and a worldview for its continued practice and application.

Final Reflection

If collective wisdom were an elixir, after a first sip we would experience an alteration of awareness and perception. Rather than being aware of problems and dividing these problems into smaller parts, we would become aware of connectedness and intricacy. We would realize that what we were seeing was not and could not be the whole picture. We would begin to scan for more information and simultaneously become curious about the perspectives of others.

With a second sip, we would experience our physical body in a new way. Rather than depending on our mind alone to solve problems or negotiate relationships, we would become aware of our heart and our gut and the symphony of feelings arising from all parts of our body. Emotions such as shame, pride, love, and anger would take on nuance and complexity; feelings would become guides to deeper self-knowledge and a way of signaling comfort or caution in relation to others.

With a third sip, hearing would be changed, and awareness of sound and vibration would be enhanced. The tones of others' voices would become as rich with meaning as their words, and their words would sound more like poetry, a necklace of ideas, thoughts, feelings, fears, and aspirations. Silence would take on as many variations as snowflakes, and each variety would have the most profound significance.

With a fourth sip, nothing would appear in isolation but rather in some form of pattern. And these patterns would have meaning and significance for action. Instead of our deciding in a typical fashion of weighing pros and cons until an answer arrived from outside one's self, a knowing would arise from inside. A confidence, born of seeking to understand patterns, would settle into the body.

With a final sip, a sharp awareness would announce itself that we are not separate from each other and that we are all needed if anything of great significance is to be accomplished.

The alterations in perception, pattern recognition, hearing, and vision, as well as a felt sense that everyone was needed, would raise new hopes and challenges. In the discovery of new and exhilarating gifts, we would know that this understanding can be used fully only if others use their gifts as well. We would become aware of the need for collective practices, of the ways that coming together can make a difference in both material and spiritual realms.

As the effects of these changes settled in, we would realize that these insights require both the light and the dark. We need the light of illumination and the darkness of incubation. We need examples that inspire hope, as well as reminders of the suffering we have faced and still face. With a breath in, we would recall that it was often in the darkest times of our own lives and in the darkest times in history that new ways, new possibilities were imagined. With a breath out, we would recall that only by finding something worthy of our efforts did we mobilize our energies and ground our determination in action. With the taste of the final sip still lingering, a calmness that was not separate from urgency would settle into our body.

It is time now that we come together.

An Invitation

If you enjoyed *The Power of Collective Wisdom* and are interested in the ideas of this book and/or meeting others who share this interest, visit our Web site at
www.thepowerofcollectivewisdom.com

Colleagues

Colleagues with Interviews, Correspondence, and Published Excerpts in this Book

(Listed in Order of Appearance)

1. Mark Gerzon
2. Angeles Arrien
3. Linda Monte
4. Carol Frenier
5. Craig Hamilton
6. Meg Wheatley
7. Peter Senge
8. Beth Jandernoa
9. Juanita Brown
10. Kate Regan
11. Paula Underwood
12. Jacob Needleman
13. Lauren Artress
14. Robert Kenny
15. Parker Palmer
16. David Potter
17. John Paul Lederach
18. David Whyte
19. Renee Levi
20. Tom Hurley
21. Barbara Nussbaum
22. Rabbi Zalman Schachter-Shalomi
23. Mona Afary
24. Daniel Goleman

Notes

Foreword

1. Peter Senge, *The Fifth Discipline: The Art and Practice of the Learning Organization* (New York: Doubleday, 2006), 370.
2. C. Otto Scharmer, *Theory U: Leading from the Future as It Emerges* (San Francisco: Berrett-Koehler Publishers, 2009). Peter Senge, C. Otto Scharmer, Joseph Jaworski, and Betty Sue Flowers, *Presence: Human Purpose and the Field of the Future* (Cambridge, MA: Society for Organizational Learning, 2004).
3. Senge, *The Fifth Discipline*, 375.

Introduction: Collective *and* Wisdom Makes the Difference

1. Gary Klein, *Sources of Power: How People Make Decisions* (Cambridge: MIT Press, 1998). See "The Best Teams: Wildland Firefighters," 236–38.
2. Mark Gerzon, correspondence with Tom Callanan, April 14, 2007.
3. George McCauley, *Journey Man* (New York: Something More Publications, 1995).

Chapter 1: What Is Collective Wisdom and How Does It Show Up?

1. Brian Meehan, "Softball Opponents Offer Unique Display of Sportsmanship," *Oregonian*, April 29, 2008, http://blog .oregonlive.com/breakingnews/2008/04/the_best_tale_of_ sportsmanship.html.
2. Angeles Arrien, interview by Alan Briskin, August 29, 2000, Sausalito, California.
3. Linda Monte, interview by Alan Briskin, September 5, 2007, South San Francisco, California.
4. Craig Hamilton, "Come Together: The Mystery of Collective Intelligence," *What Is Enlightenment?* issue 25 (May–July 2004), 58.

5. Jane Metcalfe, in Hamilton, "Come Together," 60.
6. In Juanita Brown with David Isaacs, *The World Café: Shaping Our Futures Through Conversations That Matter* (San Francisco: Berrett-Koehler Publishers, 2005).
7. Peter Senge, correspondence with Tom Callanan, October 28, 2000.
8. Beth Jandernoa, in Hamilton, "Come Together," 62.
9. Francisco J. Varela, *Ethical Know-How: Action, Wisdom, and Cognition* (Stanford: Stanford University Press, 1999).
10. Juanita Brown in Alan Briskin et al., *Centered on the Edge: Mapping a Field of Collective Intelligence and Spiritual Wisdom* (Kalamazoo, MI: Fetzer Institute, 2001).

Chapter 2: Preparing for Collective Wisdom to Arise

1. Paula Underwood, interview by Sheryl Erickson, September 7, 2000, San Anselmo, California.
2. Jacob Needleman, "Report to the Fetzer Institute in the form of a letter to Rob Lehman," March 12, 1997.
3. Needleman, *The American Soul: Rediscovering the Wisdom of the Founders* (New York: Tarcher/Putnam, 2002).
4. From Benjamin Franklin's speech to delegates of the Constitutional Convention, quoted in Needleman, *The American Soul*, 62.
5. Ibid., 63.
6. Needleman, *The American Soul*, 63–64.
7. Ibid., 65–66.
8. From Franklin's speech to delegates of the Constitutional Convention, quoted in Needleman, *The American Soul*, 67.
9. Ibid., 68.
10. Needleman, *The American Soul*, 70.
11. CBS News, "After Memorials and Prayer, Obama Joins Thousands on National Mall for Pre-Inauguration Concert," January 18, 2009, www.cbsnews.com/stories/2009/01/18/national/inauguration09/main4732505.shtml?source=RSSattr=HOME_4732505.
12. Lauren Artress, interview by Alan Briskin, September 5, 2000, San Francisco, California.
13. David Dorsey, "Positive Deviant," *Fast Company*, December 2000, 286–92.

Chapter 3: Inhabiting a Different Worldview

1. Robert Kenny, *What Scientific Research Can Teach Us About Collective Consciousness and Collective Wisdom* (Kalamazoo, MI: Collective Wisdom Initiative, 2004).
2. Laurens van der Post, *The Lost World of the Kalahari* (New York: Pyramid Books, 1966).
3. Howard W. Eves, *Mathematical Circles Adieu and Return to Mathematical Circles*, Vol. III (Washington, DC: Mathematical Association of America, 2003).
4. Parker J. Palmer, *Let Your Life Speak: Listening for the Voice of Vocation* (San Francisco: Jossey-Bass, 2000).
5. Miguel Serrano, *C. G. Jung and Hermann Hesse: A Record of Two Friendships* (New York: Schocken Books, 1966).
6. Ursula King, *Spirit of Fire: The Life and Vision of Teilhard de Chardin* (Maryknoll, NY: Orbis Books, 1996).
7. Pierre Teilhard de Chardin, "The Evolution of Chastity," in *Toward the Future* (London: William Collins Sons & Co., 1975), 86–87.
8. King, *Spirit of Fire*, 87.
9. Teilhard de Chardin, *The Phenomenon of Man* (New York: Harper and Row, 1959).
10. Ibid., 181–82.
11. Ibid., 202.
12. Mary Parker Follett, *The New State: Group Organization the Solution of Popular Government* (University Park, PA: Pennsylvania State University Press, 1998).
13. Pauline Graham, ed., *Mary Parker Follett: Prophet of Management* (Boston: Harvard Business School Press, 1996).
14. Ibid., xiii.
15. Follett, *The New State*, 230.
16. Joan C. Tonn, *Mary P. Follett: Creating Democracy, Transforming Management* (New Haven: Yale University Press, 2003).
17. Follett, *The New State*, 82.
18. Robert D. Richardson Jr., *Emerson: The Mind on Fire* (Berkeley: University of California Press, 1995).
19. Ibid., 141.
20. Ibid.
21. Ibid., 141–42.

22. Ralph Waldo Emerson, *Nature and Other Writings* (Boston: Shambhala, 2003).

Chapter 4: What Makes Groups Foolish

1. Solomon Simon, *The Wise Men of Helm and Their Merry Tales* (Springfield, NJ: Behrman House, 1942).
2. Scott Shane and Mark Mazzetti, "Ex-C.I.A. Chief, in Book, Assails Cheney on Iraq," *New York Times*, April 27, 2007, www.nytimes.com/2007/04/27/washington/27intel.html (accessed September 15, 2008).
3. Isaac Bashevis Singer, *The Fools of Chelm and Their History* (New York: Farrar, Straus, and Giroux, 1988).

Chapter 5: The Tragedy of Polarized Groups

1. Sherwin B. Nuland, *Doctors: The Biography of Medicine* (New York: Alfred A. Knopf, 1988).
2. Ibid., 250.

Chapter 6: An Illusion of Agreement

1. *In the Shadow of the Moon*, September 7, 2007, Discovery Films, Films Four, and Passion Pictures.
2. Roger Boisjoly, interview by David Potter on behalf of the Collective Wisdom Initiative, Mesquite, Nevada, August 7, 2000. Other sources include www.onlineethics.org/CMS/profpractice/exempindex/RB-intro.aspx.

Chapter 7: The Unlimited Cocreative Power of Groups and Communities

1. The Institute for Intercultural Studies, "Frequently Asked Questions About Mead/Bateson," www.interculturalstudies.org/faq.html#quote (accessed March 12, 2009).
2. Keith Sawyer, *Group Genius: The Creative Power of Collaboration* (New York: Basic Books, 2007).
3. Renee Levi, "Group Magic: An Inquiry into Experiences of Collective Resonance" (PhD diss., Saybrook Graduate School, 2003), www.resonanceproject.org/page.cfm?pt=0&id=105.

4. Angeles Arrien, interview by Alan Briskin, Sausalito, California, August 29, 2000.
5. Geoffrey Colvin, "Why Dream Teams Fail," *Fortune* (June 12, 2006), 92.
6. Tom Hurley in Briskin et al., *Centered on the Edge*, 40–41.
7. Barbara Nussbaum, interview by and correspondence with Alan Briskin, Johannesburg, South Africa. Barbara Nussbaum and Alexander Schieffer, "Dr. Taddy Blecher: A South African Social Entrepreneur Turns a New Economic Vision into Practice," World Business Academy, *Merchants of Vision* 19, issue 1 (June 23, 2005).
8. Rabbi Zalman Schachter-Shalomi, interview by Alan Briskin, Boulder, Colorado, December 10, 2004.
9. Mona Afary, interview by and correspondence with Alan Briskin, Oakland, California, August 26, 2008.
10. Daniel Goleman, *Social Intelligence: The New Science of Human Relationships* (New York: Bantam Books, 2006), 42.
11. Ibid., 43.

Chapter 8: Practices of Mindfulness for Collective Wisdom

1. Paula Underwood, interview by Sheryl Erickson, San Anselmo, California, September 7, 2000.
2. Barbara Nussbaum, "The Sound of Symphonia—What IS Working in South Africa?" Benjaminzander.com, www.benjaminzander.com/thought.asp?id=69 (accessed March 13, 2009).
3. Diana Whitney and Amanda Trosten-Bloom, *The Power of Appreciative Inquiry: A Practical Guide to Positive Change* (San Francisco: Berrett-Koehler Publishers, 2003).
4. C. Otto Scharmer, *Theory U: Leading from the Future as It Emerges* (San Francisco: Berrett-Koehler Publishers, 2009).

Acknowledgments

We want to especially acknowledge Steve Piersanti, our editor at Berrett-Koehler, who initially encouraged us to write this book and masterfully guided us every step of the way.

People who have significantly influenced our understanding and thinking about collective wisdom (teachers, mentors, guides, thinking partners, colleagues, and friends):

A. H. Almaas · Christopher Alexander · Angeles Arrien · Lauren Artress · Tom Atlee · Dick Axelrod · Emily Axelrod · Chris Bache · Ria Baeck · Rachel Bagby · Roger Benson · Wilfred Bion · Orland Bishop · Peter Block · David Bohm · David Bradford · Joanna Brown · Juanita Brown · Judy Brown · Andy Bryner · Mirabai Bush · Joseph Campbell · Barbara Cecil · Michael Cecil · Ira Chaleff · Sarita Chawla · Barry Childs · Rita Cleary · Arthur Colman · Michael Conforti · David Cooperrider · Ernie Cortez · Diane Cory · Larry Daloz · Kay Davidson · Phil Davidson · John Dicus · Anne Dosher · Elizabeth Doty · Duane Elgin · Joel Elkes · Sally Elkes · Elizabeth Faddell · Gary Ferrini · John E. Fetzer · Barbara Fields · FireHawk · Craig Fleck · Wink Franklin · Carol Frenier · Mark Friedman · Robert Fritz · Peter Garrett · Robert Gass · Glenna Gerard · Mark Gerzon · Sarah Ghiorse · Glennifer Gillespie · Bernard Glassman · Julie Glover · Michael Goodman · Gwen Gordon · Robert Greenleaf · Susan Griffin · Robert Hanig · Pat Harbour · Susan Harris · Carol Hegedus · Ron Heifetz · Bert Hellinger · David Horne · Tom Hurley · Sherry Immediato · Bill Isaacs· David Isaacs · Dennis Jaffe· Beth Jandernoa · Dadi Janki ·

Joseph Jaworski · Jon Jenkins · Peter Johnson-Lenz · Trudy Johnson-Lenz · Michael Jones · Krystyna Jurzykowski · Adam Kahane · Prasad Kaipa · Katrin Kaueffer · Will Keepin · Myron Kellner-Rogers · Robert Kenny · Charlie Kiefer · Daniel Kim · Jayanti Kirpalani · Joe Kullin · Myriam Laberge · David LaChapelle · Susan Lanier · Glen Lauder · Joan Lederman · Rob Lehman · Amy Lenzo · Renee Levi · Hanmin Liu · Jennifer Liu · Albrecht Mahr · Dawna Markova · Steve Maybury · George McCauley · Paula McFarland · Donella Meadows · Edgar Mitchell · Wayne Muller · Gayatri Naraine · Craig Neal · Patricia Neal · Jacob Needleman · Mark Nepo · Erich Neumann · Bill O'Brien · Tom Ockerse · James O'Dea · John O'Donohue · Parker Palmer · Sharon Parks · Carol Pearson · Steve Piersanti · Rose Pinard · George Por · Michael Ray · Kate Regan · Michael Regan · John Renesch · Pele Rouge · Michele Robbins · Ocean Robbins · Charlotte Roberts · Vicki Robin · Judy Rodgers · Jon Rubenstein · Teresa Ruelas · Stephanie Ryan · Mitch Saunders · Rabbi Zalman Schachter-Shalomi · Otto Scharmer · Edgar Schein · Richard Schwartz · Sandra Seagel · Peter Senge · David Sibbet · Saul Siegel · Maria Skordialos · Susan Slotter · Malidoma Somé · Melissa Spamer · Bob Stilger · Chris Strutt · Ann Svendsen ·Linda Booth Sweeney · Judith Thompson · Verneice Thompson · Howard Thurman · Justine Toms · Michael Toms · Nghia Tran · Peg Umanzio · Paula Underwood · Bill Ury · Roberto Vargas · Bill Veltrop · Marilyn Veltrop · Ursula Versteegen · Finn Voldtofte · Anne West · Meg Wheatley · Sarah Whiteley · Diana Whitney · David Whyte · Ken Wilber · Becky Winslow · Tenneson Woolf · Arthur Zajonc.

Groups of sustained inquiry of five years or longer that informed the authors' experience and contributed to this book:

Call of the Times Dialogues · Corps of Discovery · DNA of Relationships Group · Duck Club · Le Croissant Breakfast Club · Thought Leader Gatherings · Walden Pond Group.

Conferences that significantly informed the content of this book:

Mind and Life Dialogues held at MIT with the Dalai Lama: exchanges between Buddhism and the behavioral sciences on how the mind works (2003) · 3rd International Congress, Wurtzburg, Germany: Collective Wisdom: New Perspectives for Resolution in Small and Large Group Conflicts, in Families, Social Groups and in Politics (2006) · Assisi Conference: Awakening the Archetype of Wisdom (2006) · Friends (Quaker) Conference on Religion and Psychology: Group Alchemy for a New Consciousness (2008).

People who endorsed the original book proposal:

Peter Block · Juanita Brown · Dawn Engle · David Isaacs ·Joseph Jaworski · Albrecht Mahr · Peter Senge · Diana Whitney.

Colleagues responding to a survey with reflections and feedback on key ideas contained in the collective wisdom field of study and practice:

John Adams · Verna Allee · Dana Lynne Andersen · Nick Arrizza · Lauren Artress · Tom Atlee · Richard Austin · Chris Bache · Roger Benson · Eric Best · Peter Block · Martin Bonensteffe · Sue Canney ·

Robert Cannon · Nigel Catterson · Michael Cecil · Dinesh Chandra · Hazel Childs · Arthur Colman · Linda Crawford · Kay Davidson · Phil Davidson · Stephanie Davidson · Felix Doppner · Diana Durham · Andrea Dyer · Jayne Felgen · FireHawk · David Frenette · Carol Frenier · Mark Friedman · Sheryl Fullerton · Glenna Gerard · Jack Gilles · Peter Goldsbury · Pilar Gonzales · Craig Hamilton · Leilani Henry · Peggy Holman · Ken Homer · Jeff Hutner · David Issacs · Rick Jackson · Jon Jenkins · Peter Johnson-Lenz · Trudy Johnson-Lenz · Krystyna Jurzykowski · Prasad Kaipa · Marty Kaplan · Jo Ellen Koerner · Myriam Laberge · Leslie Lanes · Susan Lanier · Alexander Laszlo · Amy Lenzo · Ben Levi · Renee Levi · Bruce Lloyd · Sally Lonegren · Manuel Manga · Nancy Margulies · Renee Moorefield · Eric Nelson · Serena Newby · Carolyn North · Rose Pinard · Dave Potter · Saraswati Rain · John Renesch · Elaine Repass · Lew Rhodes · Ocean Robbins · Charlotte Roberts · Vicki Robin · Charles Savage · John Shibley · Sabine Shulte · David Sibbet · Alok Singh · Karen Speerstra · Pat McHenry Sullivan · Ann Svendsen · Tamara Trefz · Bill Veltrop · Marilyn Veltrop · Ursula Versteegen · Finn Voldtofte · Lorraine Warren · Deborah Vogele Welch · Anne West · Diana Whitney · Tenneson Woolf · Metta Zetty · Rosa Zubizarreta.

Colleagues responding to a survey with feedback on prospective titles for the book:

Maria Jesus Aguilo · Angela Anderson · Lauren Artress · Judy Asbury · Emily Axelrod · Ria Baeck · Christina Baldwin · Janice Barnett · Dawn Belardinelli · Roger Benson · Cliff Bernstein · Sue Blondell · Jan Boller · Roger Breisch · Sharon Brisnehan · Juanita

Brown · Rick Brown · Cindy Buckle · Daniel Capone · Dinesh Chandra · Sarita Chawla · Ken Chen · Joy Chiu · Laurie Chu · Jon Cleland-Host · Cristina Conchi · Donald J. Converse · Beverly Cronnelly · Michael Crowley · Haydee Cuza · Christopher De Michele · Elmar Dornberger · Elizabeth Doty · Kathleen Erickson-Freeman · Carolyn Firmin · Susan Fowler · Sheila Fusaro · B. J. Gallagher · Polly Gates · Jim Gibboney · Peter Goldsbury · John Haley · Carol Hallyn · Michael Hann · Lyn Hartley · Peggy Holman · Wade Hufford · Stella Humphries · Richard Jacobs · Robert "Jake" Jacobs · Fran Kaplan · David Kass · Bonnie Kaufman · Mary Key · John King · Lois Koteen · Bea Laney · Catherine Lengronne · Stewart Levine · Liz Linder · Bob Liss · Sally Lonegren · Kathleen Love · Mary Luttrell · Albrecht Maher · Gabriela Melano · Hamid Motamed · Craig Neal · Lauren O'Brien · Jeffery Paine · Laura Peck · Steve Piersanti · Betty Plevney · Linda Puffer · Perviz Randeria · Brad Reddersen · James Regan • Jordan Remer · John Renesch · Richard Retecki · Lew Rhodes · Angel Roberson Daniels · Charlotte Roberts · Vicki Robin · Rey Rodriguez · Teresa Ruelas · Brandon Sanders · Marta Segura · Pek Serifsoy · Katie Sheehan · Sandy Simon · Jeevan Sivasubramaniam · Carolyn Southard · Nancy Southern · Karen Speerstra · Jeanette Stokes · Anthony Suchman · Jeremy Sullivan · Pat McHenry Sullivan · Marc Tognotti · Tamara Trefz · Scott Tsunehara · Catherine Van Meter · Cassandra Vieten · Russ Volckmann · George Weissmann · Allison Wilson · Diane Wright · Leslie Yerkes · Karen Young · Arnold Zippel · Rosa Zubizarreta · Bill Zybach.

Manuscript reviewers:

Lauren Artress · Arthur Colman · Marcia Daszko · Carol Frenier · Myrna Holden · Amy Lenzo · Renee Levi · Andrea Markowitz · Steve Maybury · Craig Neal · Patricia Neal · Barbara Nussbaum · Jane O'Brien · Kate Regan · Janice Rutledge · David Sibbet · Joseph Webb · Anne West.

People who have supported and impacted the creation of this book:

Tom Beech · Dawn Belardinelli · Dick Bellin · Jan Boller · David Bradford · Alex Briskin · Carol Briskin · Chris Cahill · Rose Carino · Michelle Caughey · Ira Chaleff · Karl Chan · Joy Chiu · Gregory Coe · Lisa Ryan Cole · Rufus Cole · Arthur Colman · Colin Crabb · Bev Cronnelly · Diane Demee-Benoit · Rich Dodson · Amy Fergusson · Gary Ferrini · Annette Finkel · FireHawk · Carolyn Firmin · Rachel Flaith · Kristin Frantz · Carol Frenier · Hannah Fuchs · Martin Fuchs · Sophie Fuchs · Sheila Fusaro · Jim Gibboney · Martha Gilmore · Sheila Gilson · Terry Glubka · Linda Grdina · Cherri Glowe · Susan Harris · Guillermina Hernandez-Gallegos · Deborah Higgins · Myrna Holden · Janice Hoss · Wade Hufford · Tom Hurley · Fernanda Ibarra · Richard Jacobs · Linda Jensen · Barbara Kaplan · Marty Kaplan · Myron Kellner-Rogers · Dwane Kennedy · Jean Lathrop · Rob Lehman · Stewart Levine · Amy Lenzo · Renee Levi · Sally Lonegren · Alan Marx · Steve Maybury · Linda Monte · Hamid Motamed · Eric Nelson · Mark Nepo · Jane O'Brien · Eleanor Ott · David Palmer · Rose Pinard · Dave Potter · Ralph Reed · Kate Regan · John Renesch · Richard Retecki · Sally Retecki · Mark Riley · Sarah Robbins · Pele Rouge · Jon Rubenstein ·

Rabbi Zalman Schachter-Shalomi · Terri Seever · Shirley Showalter ·
David Sibbet · Ken Siegel · Saul Siegel · George Sinnott · Jeevan
Sivasubramaniam · Serge Teplitsky · Susan Trabucchi · Tamara
Trefz · Kim Trumbull, Scott Tsunehara · Ed Tywoniak · Peg
Umanzio ·Jean Wilhite · Becky Winslow · Jeff Wood · Jill Wood ·
Mika Yoshino · Sally Yu · Arnold Zippel.

**We want to acknowledge the entire staff of Berrett-Koehler
Publishers, who have shepherded the creation of this book in
all of its aspects.**

BOOK COVER DESIGN: Cherie Hafford and Anne West
COPYEDITING: Elissa Rabellino
PROOFREADING: Henrietta Bensussen
INDEXING: Carol Frenier
INTERIOR DESIGN: Laura Lind
INTERNET VISIBILITY: Dave Potter and Amy Lenzo
PRODUCTION: Richard Wilson and Linda Jupiter

Index

About the Collective Wisdom
Initiative

People are deeply nourished by the process of creating wholeness.

—Christopher Alexander, *The Luminous Ground: The Nature of Order*

The Collective Wisdom Initiative is an informal network of practitioners and scholars exploring an emerging field of study and practice called by its founding stewards *collective wisdom*. Initially funded through support from the Fetzer Institute in 2000, the CWI is based on the conviction that groups have the potential to be sources of extraordinary creative power, incubators of innovative ideas, and vehicles for social healing. During its initial years, the CWI was a leader in cultivating relationships across diverse disciplines, commissioning a series of groundbreaking writings, and interviewing thought leaders. The emphasis from the beginning was on the active, dynamic nature of *initiative*. There was evidence of a compelling force that was motivating people to come together in meaningful and collective ways to address social needs and concerns. In 2002, a Web site was created to make visible this emerging field.

The Web site has evolved with contributions of hundreds of people and organizations. Containing the equivalent of over two thousand pages of content, audio and video clips, and hundreds of links, the CWI is consistently number one on Google's list of over nine hundred thousand related sites. Ten "doorways" lead the visitor through the field of collective wisdom, including multimedia presentations; research from our network; maps of people, places, and events taking place around the world; and a variety of methodologies and applications.

Many of our visitors have created self-portraits of their interest and involvement in the field of collective wisdom.

We invite you to become a part of this growing social movement by visiting our site and profiling your interest in collective wisdom. Visit www.collectivewisdominitiative.org.

About the Fetzer Institute

A private foundation located in Kalamazoo, Michigan, the Fetzer Institute has given significant support to the Collective Wisdom Initiative and much of the research underlying this book. The institute's mission, to foster awareness of the power of love and forgiveness, rests on its conviction that efforts to address the critical issues facing the world must go beyond political, social, and economic strategies to their psychological and spiritual roots. The institute applies both science and spirituality to better understand the foundations of love and forgiveness, creates opportunities to bring love and forgiveness into the heart of individual and community life, and shares compelling stories that inspire others to embrace these practices. For more information, visit www.fetzer.org.

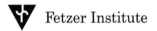 Fetzer Institute

About the Cover Image

The cover image of the spiral shell, a simple sea snail, was chosen because it speaks in three metaphorical ways to this book's themes. First, the spiral is a dynamic pattern occurring at multiple levels in nature—from the smallest chromosomes to the largest galaxies. Within many cultures, as well as within the realm of science, the spiral has come to represent growth and evolution. Similarly, collective wisdom is a naturally occurring phenomenon, revealing itself within multiple levels of society (from families to nation states), that is critical to our social growth and evolution.

Second, if we imagine navigating the spiral cavity of a shell, the path would likely be long, dark, and circuitous, with few navigational markers. Our paths forward as families, organizations, and nations can often feel similar, leading us to wonder whether we're spiraling in one direction toward wisdom or in the opposite direction toward folly. The best groups, as described in this book, develop techniques and structures for navigating away from folly and toward wisdom.

Finally, a key indicator that groups are headed in the direction of wisdom is a feeling of aliveness, coherence, simplicity, beauty—even luminousness. Our cover image embodies and radiates these same qualities that are present with collective wisdom.

In these volatile and challenging times, may the image of the humble but elegant sea snail serve as a symbol for how we might best tap our natural collective capacity and navigate our way toward greater coherence, growth, and wisdom.

About the Authors

Alan Briskin

Sheryl Erickson

John Ott

Tom Callanan

Alan Briskin is author of the award-winning book *The Stirring of Soul in the Workplace* and coauthor of *Daily Miracles*, which earned the *American Journal of Nursing*'s Book of the Year award in the category of Public Interest and Creative Works. He is coauthor of *Bringing Your Soul to Work: An Everyday Practice*. Alan is a pioneer in the field of organizational learning and co-founder of the Collective Wisdom Initiative.

His work with groups and collectives extends back to the early 1970s, when he was part of an international community in Israel founded on the principles of the communal kibbutz. As an educator, he contributed to the design of schools based on experiential learning and was the director of education for the Vermont group home that became the model for deinstitutionalization of confined youth. His interest in alternative educational settings continued for over ten years when he was the principal consultant to the George Lucas Educational Foundation.

As a health care consultant, he was a founding member of the Relationship Centered Care Network and developed programs at Kaiser Permanente for practicing physicians to deepen their communication skills with patients. He has continued for the past twenty years as a coach and mentor for physician and nurse leaders as well as an organizational consultant to executive teams, businesses, and nonprofit organizations. He serves as an adjunct faculty member at Saybrook Graduate School, where he helped design its doctoral program in organizational systems.

In corporate and conference settings, Alan has given keynotes and conducted workshops on collective wisdom throughout the United States, as well as in Canada, England, and South Africa. He has a doctorate in organizational behavior from the Wright Institute in Berkeley, California, and is a professional associate of the Grubb Institute in London. Alan lives with his wife, Jane, in Oakland, California. They have a son in college.

Visit his Web site at www.alanbriskin.com.

Sheryl Erickson has been principal investigator for the Collective Wisdom Initiative since 2000, seeking to articulate a field of study and practice now identified as that of collective wisdom.

In the late 1970s, her work was committed to creating community-based programs for low-income children and families, Head Start preschool education, and Follow Through innovative elementary education. For more than a decade, she served as a child development consultant, program evaluator, curriculum designer, and regional director of field evaluation teams.

In the mid-1980s, Sheryl transitioned from the public sector to working primarily in business with a focus on leadership development and organizational change. She was liaison for executive leadership development with Procter & Gamble (through Innovation Associates' Leadership and Mastery program), then convener and advocate for what would become a field of practice identified as organizational learning. She was instrumental in the marketing and visibility of Peter Senge's seminal management book, *The Fifth Discipline: The Art and Practice of the Learning Organization*.

With Peter Senge and an international group of practitioners, Sheryl convened the historic Bretton Woods Gathering of 1994, an innovative conference that was instrumental in catalyzing the organizational learning field. This led her to an extended period of inquiry into individual learning modalities and how groups learn and cocreate, during which she offered small group weekend explorations, online conversations, virtual cocreation projects, and large innovative gatherings. She has recently undertaken a research initiative, the Powers of Place Collaborative, looking at the relationship of place and environment to collective transformative experience.

Sheryl has an MS in human development (University of Maryland), an MA in urban elementary education (Simmons College), and an ABD in curriculum instruction and design (Boston University). She lives with her husband, Martin Fuchs, and two daughters in Massachusetts.

John Ott has designed and led successful collective change efforts for almost thirty years. He has worked with cities, counties, and large human services systems, designing and leading participatory budget processes to resolve gaping deficits. He designed and led the initial community change processes at the heart of Smart Start, a statewide initiative in North Carolina designed to ensure that every child begins kindergarten healthy and ready to succeed.

At the core of his work is a commitment to help diverse groups of people, often who have profound and contentious disagreements, learn how to create spaces of collective discernment and right action.

More recently, he has worked with mental health systems across California, bringing policy makers and service providers together with people who receive services, their families, and local community leaders to transform how mental health departments help communities promote the well-being of their members.

With his wife and partner, Rose Pinard, John led an organizational spirituality initiative funded by the Angell

Foundation. Partnering with a wide array of nonprofits, Rose and John worked to translate spiritual concepts and practices into frameworks that could help the organizations creatively address some of their most pressing challenges.

John began his work with groups as a community organizer, helping residents of communities with few economic resources to build relationships of trust and common values, discern their collective voice, and claim their power to effect change.

John holds a JD from Stanford University. He has been a lecturer of public policy studies at Duke University, helping launch the Hart Leadership Program there and serving as associate director from 1985 to 1989.

He was part of the Collective Wisdom Initiative from its earliest days and is one of the authors of *Centered on the Edge*, an early book about collective wisdom that was funded by the Fetzer Institute.

Tom Callanan is a senior advisor and former program officer at the Fetzer Institute, where he helped to cofound the Collective Wisdom Initiative (CWI) in 2000. During his time as program officer, CWI informed the projects in his portfolio with the notion that it's possible to convene groups to create greater impact than could be accomplished by anyone alone. Through his work with the institute, Tom has helped to establish a number of internationally recognized initiatives, including the following:

> *We Speak as One: Twelve Nobel Laureates Share Their Vision for Peace*: The result of a three-year project that engaged

peacemakers in developing a unified moral and spiritual voice. The laureates have since issued a global call to action based on this project. See the book and visit www .peacejam.org.

The Seasons Fund for Social Transformation: A dozen U.S. foundations are combining resources and developing shared strategies for supporting the use of personal awareness and leadership practices by those working with grassroots community change. Visit www.seasonsfund.org.

The Conflict Transformation Collaborative: Peace-building practitioners on the front lines of global conflict situations have created a global action/learning community aimed at bringing greater cooperation, visibility, and resources to the conflict transformation field. Visit www .mediatorsfoundation.org.

The Global Youth Leadership Collaborative: Young nonprofit leaders from a dozen countries are working together to build relationships and establish collaborative efforts across divides of race, class, culture, geography, religion, and nationality. Visit www.yesworld.org.

Tom is also a writer, group process facilitator, and consultant to other foundations and organizations involved in social change work. He is a former journalist, Outward Bound instructor, and mountaineer. He has three children (Bapu, Kaitlin, and Tucker) and lives in Kalamazoo, Michigan.

About Berrett-Koehler Publishers

Berrett-Koehler is an independent publisher dedicated to an ambitious mission: Creating a World That Works for All.

We believe that to truly create a better world, action is needed at all levels—individual, organizational, and societal. At the individual level, our publications help people align their lives with their values and with their aspirations for a better world. At the organizational level, our publications promote progressive leadership and management practices, socially responsible approaches to business, and humane and effective organizations. At the societal level, our publications advance social and economic justice, shared prosperity, sustainability, and new solutions to national and global issues.

A major theme of our publications is "Opening Up New Space." They challenge conventional thinking, introduce new ideas, and foster positive change. Their common quest is changing the underlying beliefs, mindsets, institutions, and structures that keep generating the same cycles of problems, no matter who our leaders are or what improvement programs we adopt.

We strive to practice what we preach—to operate our publishing company in line with the ideas in our books. At the core of our approach is stewardship, which we define as a deep sense of responsibility to administer the company for the benefit of all of our "stakeholder" groups: authors, customers, employees, investors, service providers, and the communities and environment around us.

We are grateful to the thousands of readers, authors, and other friends of the company who consider themselves to be part of the "BK Community." We hope that you, too, will join us in our mission.

Be Connected

VISIT OUR WEBSITE

Go to www.bkconnection.com to read exclusive previews and excerpts of new books, find detailed information on all Berrett-Koehler titles and authors, browse subject-area libraries of books, and get special discounts.

SUBSCRIBE TO OUR FREE E-NEWSLETTER

Be the first to hear about new publications, special discount offers, exclusive articles, news about bestsellers, and more! Get on the list for our free e-newsletter by going to www .bkconnection.com.

GET QUANTITY DISCOUNTS

Berrett-Koehler books are available at quantity discounts for orders of ten or more copies. Please call us toll-free at (800) 929-2929 or email us at bkp.orders@aidcvt.com.

HOST A READING GROUP

For tips on how to form and carry on a book reading group in your workplace or community, see our website at www .bkconnection.com.

JOIN THE BK COMMUNITY

Thousands of readers of our books have become part of the "BK Community" by participating in events featuring our authors, reviewing draft manuscripts of forthcoming books, spreading the word about their favorite books, and supporting our publishing program in other ways. If you would like to join the BK Community, please contact us at bkcommunity@bkpub.com.